"*Cold Meat Party* is hypnotically watchable, a well-made play of debate and development that might have pleased Shaw or even Priestley."

—*The Times Literary Supplement*

••

"…this is very different from Fraser's previous successes and shows a skilful maturity in its construction and a sparkling wit worthy of Coward."

—*The Stage*

••

"Brad Fraser's *Cold Meat Party* might be considered strong meat by some for some of its content, but it is brilliantly funny, cleverly structured and intensely moving in parts."

—*Clitheroe Advertiser & Times*

••

"Brad Fraser demonstrates his developing ability to juggle several theatrical styles at once, in a drawing room comedy with a dash of Agatha Christie and a nod towards Whitehall farce."

—*Lancashire Evening Post*

••

"…despite its studied outrageousness, *Cold Meat Party* is actually a good, old-fashioned, well-made play: it is tightly structured and briskly paced, the characters are for the most part convincingly drawn, and they develop during the course of the piece. Mr. Fraser handles this pheromonal vortex with deftness and panache."

—*Country Life*

••

"…it is highly entertaining, a sort of 'Big Chill' with a smack of Joe Orton and a non-stop series of carnal link-ups, revelations… rattled off in the style of 'Frasier' or 'Friends' on television."

—*Daily Mail*

COLD
meat
PARTY

Cold
Meat
Party

Brad Fraser

Playwrights Canada Press
Toronto • Canada

Playwrights Canada Press
The Canadian Drama Publisher
215 Spadina Avenue, Suite 230, Toronto, Ontario CANADA M5T 2C7
416-703-0013   fax 416-408-3402
orders@playwrightscanada.com • www.playwrightscanada.com

Financial support provided by the taxpayers of Canada and Ontario through the Canada Council for the Arts and the Department of Canadian Heritage through the Book Publishing Industry Development Programme, and the Ontario Arts Council.

The Canada Council for the Arts
Le Conseil des Arts du Canada

ONTARIO ARTS COUNCIL
CONSEIL DES ARTS DE L'ONTARIO

Front cover image: Francis Bacon, Figure with Meat, 1954 © Francis Bacon Estate/DACS/SODART 2005.
E12892 Francis Bacon, British, 1909-1992, Figure with Meat, 1954, oil on canvas, 50 7/8 x 48 in. (129.9 x 121.9 cm), Harriott A. Fox Fund, 1956.1201 Reproduction, The Art Institute of Chicago.
Production Editor/Cover design: JLArt

Library and Archives Canada Cataloguing in Publication

Fraser, Brad, 1959-
Cold meat party / Brad Fraser.

A play.

ISBN 0-88754-786-9

I. Title.

PS8561.R294C64 2006   C812'.54   C2006-900610-5

First edition: March 2006.
Printed and bound by AGMV Marquis at Quebec, Canada.

This play is dedicated to Braham Murray, the best midwife ever.

Acknowledgements

The playwright wishes to acknowledge the many talented professionals at Canstage in Toronto and the Royal Exchange Theatre in Manchester, England who took part in the development of this play. Their contributions were invaluable and greatly appreciated. I would also like to acknowledge Factory Theatre Artistic Director Ken Gass, who had the balls.

Cold Meat Party premiered at the Royal Exchange Theatre, Manchester, England, in March 2003, with the following company:

NASH	Geraldine Alexander
FRITZ	Helen Atkinson Wood
AMANDA	Kellie Bright
NANCY	Emma Lowndes
MARCUS	Colin Tierney
DEAN	Tom Hodgkins
BRYNN	Joseph Millson

Directed by Braham Murray
Designed by Liz Ascroft
Lighting by Bruno Poet
Sound by Steve Brown
Assistant Director: Joanna Combes
Stage Manager: Jamie Byron
Deputy Stage Manager: Tracey Fleet
Assistant Stage Manager: Emma Bleaney

• • •

Cold Meat Party had its Canadian premiere at Factory Theatre, Toronto, in September 2004, with the following company:

NASH	Sarah Orenstein
FRITZ	Cherilee Garofano
AMANDA	Amy Price-Francis
NANCY	Erin Mackinnon
MARCUS	Ross Manson
DEAN	Ron White
BRYNN	James Gallander

Directed by Braham Murray
Designed by Astrid Janson
Lighting Designed by Bonnie Beecher

A Note on Punctuation

Grammatically, the dictates of dialogue, particularly dialogue that is meant to be spoken aloud rather than read silently, is a challenge for the playwright. On one hand editors, teachers, and academics all love to have rules that they expect everyone to follow even though those rules are often inconsistent and, in some cases, completely wrong. On the other hand are the writers, performers, and casual readers who prefer dialogue that constantly moves forward, and who, frankly, could care less about the proper use and improper abuse of the humble comma. I am of the mind that spoken dialogue should only be punctuated, and rarely, with the odd dash.

I believe this because when my work is performed, I want to hear the characters thoughts. I don't want to hear the writer or editor's punctuation. But the truth is, if you use punctuation you will certainly hear it in performance. It can't be helped. It's too deeply ingrained in the way we learn to read, both silently and aloud. If there is a comma in the line you will hear a comma in the delivery. It has everything to do with the way we read and nothing at all to do with the way we speak.

In natural, everyday conversation that follows the often disorderly flow of our thoughts there are no commas. Even periods and question marks appear only infrequently. One never uses a semicolon or colon in conversation. I have, as a writer, struggled from the beginning of my career to find what will, hopefully, one day be the perfect compromise with the way people actually speak and the way we must make them speak on the stage or screen in order to make their thoughts coherent. This is not an easy task and it has demanded that I be as creative with my use of punctuation as I am with words. For certain readers this can be a bit confusing.

For example, in *Snake in Fridge,* with the exception of the occasional dash, there is no internal punctuation at all. I chose this—much to the chagrin of editors and publishers everywhere—because the worldly lexicon of *Snake* never stops, never pauses, never falters. It is a roller coaster of language—there are fast parts and there are slow parts, but there are no stops—even the pauses are filled with forward thrusting action. The language of *Snake* should not be treated as the language of any literary form. It is live. I believe its lack of punctuation, the fact that the reader and the performer must often speak a line aloud in order to understand it, contributes to the energy and the challenge of that play.

Cold Meat Party is a slightly different animal. It is a more formal play. The characters are older. Their general experience and education level is higher. They are a more academic crowd. They do occasionally speak with commas. But they still don't speak with as many commas as the characters in a novelistic construction. The rules of punctuation in *Cold Meat Party* are not the rules of prose.

They are the rules of the playwright trying to find a workable balance between the truth of a character's way of speaking and a representation of that speech that is understandable on the printed page. But most of all, the punctuation has been used in a way that will least impede the forward movement of both word and thought. It can be odd. It can even be confusing. But if you speak the words out loud, the way an actor would, to another character with a strong objective in mind, I think you will understand exactly what I mean.

—*BF*

Characters

Nash Proctor	Forty-three. Canadian. Female.
Marcus Rogers	Forty-two. Canadian. Male.
Dean Turnbull	Forty-three. Canadian. Male.
Nancy Proctor	Nineteen. Canadian. Female.
Brynn (Brin) Peacock	Thirty-three. British. Male.
Fritz Harris	Thirty-five. American. Female.
Amanda Spencer	Twenty-five. British. Female.

Setting

A bed and breakfast establishment in Manchester, England. A single room represents the many identical bedrooms in the old, converted house. The bedroom has two doors, one leading to the corridor and one leading to the adjoining bathroom. There is a large common area that functions as both living and dining rooms. There are a number of doors leading from this room to other parts of the house. There is a large coffin in the centre of the common room.

Cold Meat Party

Act One

> *Lights rise on the living area of the bed and breakfast. NASH stands next to the coffin, with one hand resting on it. NANCY enters.*

NANCY   Got us both unpacked.

NASH   You hung my clothes up properly?

NANCY   Of course.

NASH   Thank you. That top's a very good choice.

NANCY   Thank you.

NASH   I'm not sure about that lipstick though.

NANCY   Mother—

NASH   The top is stunning.

> *NANCY moves to the coffin.*

NANCY   Dead people are so weird.

NASH   He was very special.

NANCY   Can't prove it by me.

NASH   You know I thought it would be too confusing to have Keith waltzing in and out of your life at irregular intervals. Are you resentful?

NANCY   We went through that whole thing when I was sixteen and hated you.

NASH   Yes. I still remember that.

NANCY   All girls hate their mothers for at least two years in their teens. It's important.

NASH	But still—there might be hidden resentments—suppressed feelings of paternal abandonment—
NANCY	He's just another dead old guy to me.
NASH	He was a marvellous writer.
NANCY	Who cares?
NASH	If you'd read just one of his books—
NANCY	*(cutting her off)* No thanks. How are you?
NASH	I'm not sure. How are the rooms?
NANCY	Nice. They're all exactly the same but a different colour. Our names are on cards on the doors. Your room is yellow. Mine is red.
NASH	Nancy, he was your father—
NANCY	Mom, leave it alone.

MARCUS and BRYNN enter with luggage.

MARCUS	Nash?
NASH	Marcus.

Pause.

MARCUS	You look great.
NASH	You too.

They embrace and kiss.

Been a while, buddy.

MARCUS	Too long.
NANCY	Ahem.
NASH	You remember Nancy.
MARCUS	You've grown up. A lot.
NANCY	I just love "Buzz Saw Affection." It's my favourite classic song of all time.
MARCUS	Of course it is. Old school, right? Nash, Nancy, this is my partner, Brynn.

NASH	Hey Brynn.
NANCY	Hi.
BRYNN	Ladies.

Pause.

MARCUS	So this is the place.
NASH	Where Keith spent his final years.
MARCUS	And his coffin. How dramatic.
NASH	I wonder why the casket's closed.
NANCY	Maybe he's starting to smell.
MARCUS	He doesn't want us to see how he's aged.
NASH	Vain bastard.
MARCUS	When did you get in?
NASH	Half an hour ago.
MARCUS	Is there anyone here?
NANCY	Not so far.

AMANDA enters.

AMANDA	You are here!
NASH	You must be Amanda.
AMANDA	Yes I'm bloody Amanda. I've been at the airport all morning waiting for your flights to arrive. Did no one see me waving this little sign that says Keith's Friends?
NASH	No. There were a great many people waving little signs.
NANCY	It gives her a headache.
AMANDA	I said on the fax that I'd meet you all at the airport.
MARCUS	Faxes always say that. It's almost never true. Especially in Russia.
NASH	Sorry. I completely misunderstood. We did find a key under the mat.

MARCUS	We came through Amsterdam last night and stayed at the Mal Maison.
AMANDA	At least someone waited for me.
NASH/ MARCUS	Dean.

DEAN enters with luggage.

DEAN	Hello.
NASH	Dean.

NASH and DEAN cheek-kiss stiffly.

Where are Kelly and the girls?

DEAN	Stayed home. The girls graduate in two weeks and Kelly never knew Keith.
NASH	They're well?
DEAN	Very.
NASH	Good. This is Nancy.
DEAN	Hello. Hi Marcus.
MARCUS	Hey Dean.
DEAN	Not even a handshake?
MARCUS	I assumed you wouldn't want to touch me.

Pause.

AMANDA	I'll make tea.

AMANDA exits.

DEAN	Marcus. Come on.
MARCUS	All right—but don't linger.

DEAN goes to MARCUS and embraces him manfully.

This is my—lover Brynn.

DEAN	Brynn.

BRYNN ignores DEAN's offered hand.

Gentlemen, we're here to honour a friend. Our political differences shouldn't ruin that.

BRYNN   Shouldn't they?

MARCUS   This is so like Keith Andrews. Always having to be the centre of attention.

NASH   I think those who die have earned the spotlight for at least a moment.

DEAN   Like Keith ever lacked for spotlight.

MARCUS   I've enjoyed a bit of spotlight myself.

DEAN   Maybe he didn't have the intensity of your success, Marcus but he certainly shone for a very long time.

NASH   *The New York Times* even ran his obit.

MARCUS   I'm sure *The New York Times* will run my obit too.

BRYNN   I think it already has.

MARCUS   Funny.

NASH   Keith certainly made the most money.

BRYNN   He was awfully good.

DEAN   I read the one about the foot fetish guy on the plane. *Stiletto Heels.* A little too wild for my tastes.

MARCUS   Didn't keep you from reading it though.

DEAN   I read everything Keith wrote.

BRYNN   Me too. I thought he was brilliant.

MARCUS   Really?

BRYNN   Yes.

MARCUS   You never told me that.

BRYNN   No?

DEAN   Nash, I could see his influence in your last film.

NASH   How do you know it wasn't me influencing him?

NANCY   Cool. A gay pop star, a feminist filmmaker and a homophobic politician at the same funeral.

DEAN   I'm really not homophobic.

NASH   I'm not really a feminist.

MARCUS   I'm not really a pop star.

BRYNN   How can you say you're not homophobic?

DEAN   I'm not as extreme as the press might have you believe.

NASH   None of us are.

MARCUS   Touché.

DEAN   I'm sure I don't have to tell either of you how easy it is for the media to reduce an argument or opinion to the most basic level.

BRYNN   Especially when that argument or opinion is already outdated and invalid to begin with.

NASH   Now boys, don't make me confine you to your trailers until we're ready to shoot. It's a friendly gathering.

NANCY   This is so "Big Chill."

                    AMANDA enters with tea.

AMANDA   Tea.

NANCY   Thanks.

NASH   It's sad we never got to see Keith here while he was alive.

DEAN   It's quite the place.

MARCUS   What was he doing when he died?

AMANDA   Drinking bourbon, smoking a cigarette and talking about himself.

NASH   At least he died happy.

MARCUS   Who expects to blow a blood vessel in their brain at forty-five?

NASH   At least it was quick.

BRYNN   No time to plan.

MARCUS   We should all be so lucky.

DEAN	He must've had some idea—he did arrange our coming with his lawyer.
AMANDA	These arrangements were made a while ago. In the eventuality of his death.
NASH	Amanda, why's the coffin closed?
AMANDA	He wanted you all to remember him as he was in life.
MARCUS	I knew it. But he still had to be here.
DEAN	He hated to miss a party.
NANCY	Closed is just fine with me. Who wants to spend the weekend looking at a corpse?

FRITZ enters with luggage.

FRITZ	Hello.

Short pause.

MARCUS	Hello.
FRITZ	I'm Fritz.

Short pause.

MARCUS	So?
FRITZ	You're Marcus Rogers.
MARCUS	Guilty.
FRITZ	You haven't changed since the first time I saw you on "Solid Gold."
MARCUS	Thanks—who the hell are you?
FRITZ	Fritz Harris. I'm an old friend of Keith's.
BRYNN	Hi.
NANCY	Hi. Nancy. Nash is my mother. Keith was my father. But only in the biological sense.
NASH	An old friend?
FRITZ	He never mentioned me to any of you?
DEAN	Where are you from, Fritz?

FRITZ	Cincinnati.
MARCUS	Fritz from Cincinnati?
	Short pause.
NASH	No.
AMANDA	I called all of the people he specified.
FRITZ	Oh he probably wouldn't have specified me. It was a very long time ago and very—transitory.
DEAN	I'm Dean, Fritz.
FRITZ	Keith told me all about you. I understand you're doing quite well in politics these days.
BRYNN	He's the next Margaret Thatcher.
FRITZ	You must be homosexual.
BRYNN	Brynn Peacock. Marcus's—partner.
FRITZ	And the infamous Nash Proctor. This is an honour.
NASH	Really?
FRITZ	Keith and I watched "Another Meat Butterfly" together when it first came out. I was very impressed. An accomplished sophomore effort I thought.
NASH	Thanks.
FRITZ	And Marcus I know "Buzz Saw Affection" is your biggest hit but I hope you won't mind if I agree with Keith and say that you brashest work was when you were with Martha Raygun and the Vaginal Booga Things.
MARCUS	Jesus no one remembers Martha Raygun and the Vaginal Booga Things.
NANCY	Was that your first band?
NASH	A punk group he had in college.
MARCUS	We changed our name to Martha and the Vadges after some feminists threatened to kill us when our first album came out. You must be quite the connoisseur—it was only issued once—on vinyl.

FRITZ	I found it in a second-hand record shop, Marc.
MARCUS	Please feel free to call me Marcus.
FRITZ	Of course. Forgive my presumption. It's so easy to be familiar with people whose work you've known for so long. I'm exhausted. And sad. Keith wrote me when he bought this place. He said there'd always be a room for me.
AMANDA	Did he now?
FRITZ	Is it a problem?

Pause.

AMANDA	Take one of the rooms that doesn't have a name card on the door.
FRITZ	Thank you. Excuse me. I'm sure we'll all be able to get to know one another better at dinner.

FRITZ exits.

BRYNN	I'll unpack our things.

BRYNN exits.

MARCUS	I don't believe in women named Fritz.
AMANDA	Cincinnati's in Ontario right?
NANCY	Ohio wrong.
NASH	What if she's some stalker or demented fan? How do we know she even knew him?
DEAN	How else would she know such intimate details of our lives?
MARCUS	Intimate details?
NASH	She could find any of that information on the Internet.
DEAN	Is it so hard to believe Keith loved people other than us?
MARCUS	Yes.
DEAN	Give the poor woman a break. She's obviously harmless. Excuse me.

DEAN exits with his suitcase.

AMANDA	I'll show you to your room.

AMANDA exits after DEAN.

NANCY   I'm gonna take a shower. I smell like airplane sweat.

NANCY exits.

NASH   Jet-lagged?

MARCUS   I'm used to it.

NASH   Seems like I'm always on an airplane. And flying's not what it used to be.

MARCUS   Nothing's what it used to be since the—skyscraper thing.

NASH   It's hell living in a constant state of uncertainty. Nancy thinks I should take anti-anxiety drugs to fly.

MARCUS   She's beautiful.

NASH   In some ways she's my best friend.

MARCUS   How handy to give birth to your own best friend.

NASH   She starts university next fall.

MARCUS   Taking?

NASH   Pre-med.

MARCUS   Impressive.

NASH   How long have you and Handsome Boy been together?

MARCUS   Four years. I got tired of pursuing freelance pointy-oink and decided to get something regular.

NASH   Four years. Really?

MARCUS   Really. The world's rotating faster or something. Time's speeding up. Think there's a drink around here?

NASH   Check the sideboard.

MARCUS   Of course. Would you like something? Or are you still not drinking?

NASH   Still not drinking.

MARCUS   Good for you.

NASH   I thought you were not drinking these days.

MARCUS	No, I'm actually not taking drugs these days. I am not drinking heavily these days.
NASH	You don't have trouble controlling it?
MARCUS	Sure. But if I become an alcoholic I'll have to quit drinking and I couldn't face that. Did you do the AA thing?
NASH	No. I woke up one morning, I had a bleeding nose, there were four unknown men in my bed and I was wearing a turban.
MARCUS	A turban? Eew.
NASH	Exactly. It was time to stop. And so I did. It nearly killed me but I did it.
MARCUS	Good for you. Pop?
NASH	Ginger ale?
MARCUS	Coke.
NASH	Coke.
MARCUS	A toast?
NASH	To Keith?
MARCUS	To all of us. And our many successes.
NASH	And Keith. I'll miss his laugh.
MARCUS	I'll miss his hands. He had the thickest hands.
NASH	With all that lovely black hair around the wrists.
MARCUS	Yes.

Pause.

	I did think the books started to get formulaic after ninety-five though. They lost their—abrasion.
NASH	I read a review of your last album that said the same thing.
MARCUS	Thanks. Bitch.
NASH	My reviews haven't been that great either.
MARCUS	At least Keith made a fortune.
NASH	When was the last time you saw him?

MARCUS	We met in ninety-eight when I was doing a benefit in London. Had too much to drink talked about old times I came onto him he rejected me I told him I hated him and never wanted to see him again and stormed out of the bar and puked in the gutter and woke up in my hotel room feeling like death. Who would've thought the bastard would have the bad taste to die before we had a chance to make up. And you?
NASH	I met him in Vancouver a few years ago. He wanted to see Nancy. Nancy didn't want to see him.
MARCUS	Resentful?
NASH	Indifferent. She was curious about him when she was a girl but as she got older she just seemed to—lose interest.
MARCUS	It's hard for kids to not have fathers.
NASH	We learn to live with it. What's your take on Dean?
MARCUS	He's finally become the person he always threatened to be.
NASH	I knew he was uptight but I had no idea…
MARCUS	Does he still make you horny, Nash?
NASH	Marcus, please!
MARCUS	He's aged well.
NASH	He has.
MARCUS	And there was that time—
NASH	*(cuts him off)* Let's not start regurgitating ancient history, pal.
MARCUS	Of course.
	Pause.
NASH	You still mad at me?
MARCUS	For abandoning me?
NASH	It's different when you have a kid. You stop thinking of yourself so much.
MARCUS	And everyone else too.

NASH	I couldn't exactly be one of the guys while I was pregnant.
MARCUS	It took me a year to realize you'd cut me off. Had I known about your new best friend I might've understood.
NASH	I really did miss you.
MARCUS	Good.

> *Lights rise on MARCUS and BRYNN's bedroom. BRYNN is unpacking. The door is open. NANCY knocks and enters. She wears a robe and dries her hair.*

NANCY	There's something wrong with that shower. You get a sort of watering-can effect.
BRYNN	You'll find most of the showers in England are like that.
NANCY	And what kinda third world country is it when you can't get hot and cold water to come out of the tap at the same time?
BRYNN	Careful. The English have very little patience with whiny North American tourists. They want your money and they want you to keep your mouth shut.
NANCY	We're not tourists we're mourners. *(She tests the bounce of his bed.)* Not bad, eh?
BRYNN	Quite nice.
NANCY	The lavender room. Figures. Are you from Manchester?
BRYNN	London.
NANCY	Must be great to come back home.
BRYNN	Not particularly—no.
NANCY	But this is England. You invented like everything.
BRYNN	England pays a lot of attention to its rules and traditions.
NANCY	What's it like being Marcus Rogers's lover?
BRYNN	You're rather young to be so interested in his music.
NANCY	Mom played it. I liked it.
BRYNN	You're not impressed by his fame?

NANCY	Please. Mostly morons get famous. Who else would want it?
BRYNN	It's an accomplishment.
NANCY	It's luck. Trust me. I've watched my mother flirt with it all my life. And she's only a moderate success.
BRYNN	I've never seen much to recommend it.
NANCY	She claims she's not interested in public attention—but you don't make your first feature about a magical talking tampon if you're not looking for attention.
BRYNN	I watched "Red Tip" with Marcus. It was very funny.
NANCY	You don't seem gay.
BRYNN	I find the labelling of sexuality middle-class and repressive.
NANCY	You sound like one of those fags who just can't admit they're fags.
BRYNN	I enjoy women as well.
NANCY	So you're bi.
BRYNN	I'm me.
NANCY	I want to be bisexual only it's so trendy y'know. I think about it a lot because so many guys are so creepy and so many girls are so cool. I think I respond biologically to men though.
BRYNN	I don't believe in the tyranny of innate sexual persuasion.

MARCUS enters.

MARCUS	Hello.
NANCY	I didn't know your boyfriend was bi.
BRYNN	I'm not bi.
MARCUS	He doesn't believe in labels. He's bi.
BRYNN	I'm in love with Marcus. That's all that matters.
NANCY	*(to MARCUS)* Does he work?
MARCUS	Brynn is notorious in the catering world.
BRYNN	I'm adept at serving people.

NANCY	Great. See ya later guys.

NANCY exits.

MARCUS	Definitely her mother's daughter.
BRYNN	Just how close are you to the mother?
MARCUS	Very close. But that was a long time ago.
BRYNN	I sensed some retro-tension.
MARCUS	Best friends. Both in love with the same man she has his baby I don't take it well blah blah blah. Where's the laptop?
BRYNN	Right there. The adapter's in the case.
MARCUS	I need to see if there's an email from the record company.
BRYNN	It's too soon.
MARCUS	It's five hours later here.
BRYNN	Yes, but time's still the same in North America.
MARCUS	Do I need a special plug for the phone jack?
BRYNN	It's in the case. Did you sleep with her?
MARCUS	Me, Dean and Keith.
BRYNN	All together?
MARCUS	Once.
BRYNN	Surely you didn't get the puritanical Mr. Turnbull to indulge in some male-on-male horseplay?
MARCUS	He mostly just watched.
BRYNN	Marcus, I didn't know you had it in you.
MARCUS	It was the eighties. We all had it in us. I didn't realize you'd read all of Keith's books.
BRYNN	It never came up.
MARCUS	You knew he was my friend.
BRYNN	I thought you'd tell me about him when you were ready.
MARCUS	Our friendship was complicated. We fought as much as we got along.

BRYNN   I understand.

> *Pause.*

MARCUS   Are you planning to visit any family or anything while we're—

BRYNN   *(cutting him off)* No.

MARCUS   Okay.

> *A light rises on AMANDA in the dining room, setting the table. NANCY enters.*

NANCY   You need a hand?

AMANDA   Oh no. I'm almost done now thanks.

NANCY   Are you from Manchester?

AMANDA   Born and bred.

NANCY   You're the first English person I've seen with real teeth.

AMANDA   I've always felt that Americans all have teeth that look like they bought them in Disneyland.

NANCY   You do know that Canada and America are different countries right?

AMANDA   The only thing I really know about Canadians is that they're supposed to be boring.

NANCY   Four words. Prince Charles Cliff Richard. What do you do for a living?

AMANDA   I'm a secretary.

NANCY   What's that like?

AMANDA   A slow creeping death. Do you work?

NANCY   I'm registered for university. Pre-med.

AMANDA   Will you specialize?

NANCY   I haven't decided. I'm not—never tell your mother you want to be a doctor when you're twelve years old—she'll hold you to it for the rest of your life.

AMANDA   There are worse fates.

NANCY	Do you plan to go to school?
AMANDA	I could never afford it.
NANCY	It costs a bundle and—I'm trying to think of a subtle way to let Mom know I'm considering taking a few years off to travel.
AMANDA	You sound uncertain.
NANCY	She wants this way more than I do. Did you get time off work for all of this?
AMANDA	No. We weren't married so—there's no bereavement—no—

Short pause as AMANDA breaks off, upset.

NANCY	Do you need anything? Can I go to the liquor store or something for you?
AMANDA	No. Sorry.
NANCY	Okay. Great. Bye.

NANCY exits. Lights rise on DEAN's bedroom. He is neatly unpacking his neatly-folded clothes. His door opens and FRITZ enters. DEAN stops unpacking. They stare at one another for a moment.

DEAN	Fritz?
FRITZ	It's a great name.
DEAN	Why call attention to yourself like that? Why not Brenda or Linda or Sally? Those are nice non-attention-getting names.
FRITZ	Am I what you expected?
DEAN	Well you smell a little differently—
FRITZ	Unpleasant?
DEAN	Just different than I expected.
FRITZ	You're slightly heavier than your JPEG.
DEAN	It's a couple years old.
FRITZ	It might be the resolution on my monitor. You're sure you're ready?

Pause.

DEAN	I'm ready.
FRITZ	You've taken care of your schedule?
DEAN	Yes. I've added on an extra four days at a Premier Lodge. Please try to keep a low profile until the others are gone.
FRITZ	They're an impressive group.
DEAN	They're just people like everyone else.
FRITZ	Well-known people.
DEAN	They're my friends. They're not stupid. We have to be careful.
FRITZ	Why is it you were the only one who didn't become a successful artist?
DEAN	I'm not artistic!
FRITZ	Okay. Clear on that.
DEAN	I don't know why you had to come here. You could've stayed in a hotel just as easily.
FRITZ	If there's no personal connection I can't do it.
DEAN	Did you bring the—what's necessary?
FRITZ	Hardly. It might be a bit embarrassing at customs.
DEAN	Right.
FRITZ	They're not as casual as they used to be. I've made arrangements here.
DEAN	Good.
FRITZ	And after the funeral—just the two of us.
DEAN	Yes.

> *FRITZ exits. Lights fade to black. There is the chiming of a small crystal bell. Lights rise on the dining room. AMANDA enters carrying a large serving dish, which she sets in the middle of the table. NANCY enters.*

NANCY	You need a hand now?
AMANDA	All right then. In the kitchen.

NANCY	It doesn't involve cooking does it?
AMANDA	No.
NANCY	Good. I really only cook with the phone.

They exit to the kitchen. DEAN and NASH enter.

DEAN	Did you nap?
NASH	Tried. I couldn't stop thinking about Keith.
DEAN	Me too.
NASH	I—it's hard to accept. He was so young. Vital. He seemed—eternal.
DEAN	I never really thought of his move to England as a permanent thing.
NASH	I know what you mean. It seemed like a phase.

AMANDA and NANCY enter with dishes.

NANCY	I'm helping.
AMANDA	I'm doing this today and I'll do it again on Sunday. Other than that you're on your own.
NASH	Amanda, do you secretly resent us?
AMANDA	Come and go as you please but don't expect me to wait on you.
NANCY	I walked up to the High Street.
NASH	Nancy, it's not a good idea to go out into a strange city without a guide.
NANCY	What did you want me to do? Hire a Sherpa?
NASH	Sweetie, I want to experience this with you.
NANCY	Hello. You were sleeping.
NASH	You should've called me.
NANCY	Didn't think of it.
AMANDA	I've assumed everyone will have wine.
DEAN	None for me thanks.

NASH	Or me.
NANCY	It's a nice city. Like Calgary only with history and interesting people. A Rastafarian winked at me.

BRYNN and MARCUS enter.

MARCUS	Something smells heavenly.
NANCY	I went to Piccadilly. I think that's where the drug dealers hang out.
MARCUS	I don't suppose you managed to score some reefer?
NANCY	Um—no.
MARCUS	Why do people have children if they're not going to teach them anything useful?
BRYNN	Ignore him. He doesn't even smoke pot anymore.
MARCUS	I used to. Lots. I never knew what was real. It was lovely.

FRITZ enters.

FRITZ	This is really a beautiful old place. The décor is so tasteful. And green is such a daring colour choice for a room.
AMANDA	Help yourself.
DEAN	Amanda, how long did you know Keith?
AMANDA	I met him at a reading at the library four years ago. I was a great admirer of his.
NASH	I'm sure he was a great admirer of yours as well.
AMANDA	I wasn't much of a reader but someone lent me *Little Girl Snatch* and it was so good I had to meet him.
FRITZ	And you had things in common?
AMANDA	He mentioned he was looking for someone to help him with the bed and breakfast and I mentioned I was looking for part-time work and—well here I am.
NASH	So you're an employee.
AMANDA	We got close.
MARCUS	Very close?

AMANDA	Close enough. He spoke of all of you often.
MARCUS	Did he ever tell you about the time Dean got so drunk he lost his shoes in a taxi?
AMANDA	No.
DEAN	It's true. I was a drunk. I'm not ashamed of it.
NASH	I'm not ashamed of having been a drunk. I'm just ashamed of about a thousand things I've done when I was drunk.
MARCUS	I am occasionally retroactively embarrassed. Were we all drunk the night we had that group thing?
NASH	Oh yeah.
DEAN	Whenever I crave another drink I think of that time.
NASH	Do you burn with shame or get an erection?
MARCUS	Careful darling, your daughter's in the room.
NANCY	Oh please. Who do you think undressed her and got her into bed every night when she was drinking? You should've seen some of the men she dragged home. Bow-wow.
NASH	Clean for five years.
NANCY	Polluted for thirty something.
DEAN	Amanda, this is really very good.
BRYNN	An abundance of flavour for English food.
AMANDA	Thanks. Fritz, I'm curious—how did you know Keith's best friends would arrive here now?
FRITZ	I didn't. But when I read about his death I—well, I just thought I'd come. I don't know why really. I couldn't stop thinking about him.
NASH	So you knew him well?
FRITZ	I knew him intensely. He was in Cincinnati for a reading.
DEAN	Am I detecting a pattern here?
FRITZ	I had to come. For closure.
DEAN	Of course—closure. Closure.

FRITZ I can leave if you want me to. But it makes me feel so much better to be with people who knew him—who loved him.

DEAN I don't think that'll be necessary. Unless Amanda's promised your room to someone else.

AMANDA I cancelled all the reservations.

DEAN So you're not inconveniencing anyone.

> *MARCUS's timer goes off with a soft beep. He turns it off, takes a pill container out of a pocket and takes a number of pills. The others try not to watch.*

MARCUS We're not going to have desperate fans showing up and trying to steal things or anything like that are we?

AMANDA I don't think so. Keith protected his address and other personal information from the "fans."

DEAN I'm sure he did.

NASH Especially after that nasty stalking incident with the no-neck woman.

MARCUS Booga Booga the no-neck woman.

DEAN She actually showed up inside his house in the middle of the night claiming he'd ripped off her life for this first novel.

NASH She was a fool. Everyone knows it was my life he ripped off for his first novel.

DEAN Do you think she's why he came here?

NASH I know he wasn't really happy in Canada those last few years but I can hardly see him letting the no-neck woman drive him out.

AMANDA He told me North America was an uptight virgin who was about to get gangbanged by the third world and he didn't want to be around for it.

BRYNN So move to Britain where we're so used to getting banged by our neighbours it's a way of life.

> *MARCUS chokes on a pill, coughing.*

Do you need more water?

MARCUS	I'm okay.
NANCY	Do you have AIDS?
MARCUS	I'm HIV-positive.

Pause.

Everyone knew that—right?

NASH	Of course.
NANCY	I guess I did read it but I forgot.
DEAN	Marcus, I had no idea. Are there—uh—any special precautions the rest of us need to take to protect ourselves?
BRYNN	Don't ingest any of his blood or semen.

Pause.

DEAN	That's—easy enough.
AMANDA	Tea?
NASH	Nancy, offer to help Amanda clear up.
NANCY	I thought we could both lend a hand.
NASH	I guess the men'll be washing dishes.
NANCY	I think so.
BRYNN	I'll take care of them. I like to wash things.
NANCY	You're strange.
FRITZ	I think the way you've raised the profile of healthy people living with HIV has been highly commendable.
MARCUS	Thank you.
BRYNN	You know a great many multi-syllabic words for someone from Cincinnati.
FRITZ	Keith wasn't the only writer in this group.
AMANDA	Do you write fiction too?
FRITZ	No. Non-fiction.
MARCUS	Say what?
NASH	What sort of non-fiction?

FRITZ	I do—journalistic stuff mostly.
	Pause.
NASH	What sort of—journalistic stuff?
FRITZ	I'm a financial writer.
MARCUS	Okay then.
NASH	That's different.
DEAN	Financial writers aren't even really journalists.
MARCUS	As long as you're not some muckraking Judas who's going to write mean things about us.
FRITZ	I'm here for the same reasons you are.
AMANDA	Keith always said his friends were a talented group of people but I really had no idea.
FRITZ	Well, I certainly wouldn't compare myself to Keith Andrews or Nash Proctor or Marcus Rogers—
AMANDA	I know exactly what you mean. It's boring having no talent isn't it?
FRITZ	I didn't actually say that I have no talent.
DEAN	You don't have to tell me how frustrating it is to hang around with creative people when you have no creativity yourself.
FRITZ	I didn't say I have no creativity—
BRYNN	But helping the talented people is a talent in itself.
AMANDA	Everything's always about helping out the talented one.
NANCY	They always think they're better than everybody else.
DEAN	I have no real talent.
BRYNN	We know that.
AMANDA	I made some trifle.
MARCUS	No dessert thanks.
BRYNN	I'll have to pass as well.
NASH	Count me out.

NANCY	Amanda, I'll have twice as much as everyone else.
AMANDA	It's nice to see not all North Americans are weight-obsessed.
NANCY	I'm just gonna puke it up anyway.
NASH	Nancy.
NANCY	Kidding.
MARCUS	I'm not weight-obsessed—I'm fat.
NASH	You're not fat.
DEAN	You don't look much different than you did in university. Well you did wear eyeliner then.
MARCUS	I'm wearing eyeliner now. I'm just better at applying it.
NANCY	I'll help you get that, Amanda.

NANCY and AMANDA exit. Pause.

MARCUS	Okay is it just me or is everyone else also wondering what Keith was doing with her?
DEAN	She is a bit young.
MARCUS	And a bit—brusque.
BRYNN	She's entertaining her lover's oldest friends. It's bound to be unsettling.
NASH	I don't think we should assume they were lovers.
MARCUS	We're talking about Keith. Of course they were lovers.
DEAN	Marcus, you haven't had a new album out for a long time.
MARCUS	They're releasing it in North America today.
NASH	Really?
FRITZ	I haven't read a thing about it.
BRYNN	That's a bit of a problem.
MARCUS	When I was twenty-eight the press waited outside my house to see what I'd wear. Now they wouldn't come by if I offered free drinks, a hot lunch and a hum job. Coming to England was better than dealing with the press—or lack thereof.

FRITZ I look forward to all of your albums.

MARCUS You're starting to just slightly creep me out.

DEAN And what about you, Nash?

NASH A couple things in development. And you?

MARCUS Any human rights you've violated lately?

NASH Small talk, buddy.

BRYNN So far you've defended a Christian college for firing a gay professor—

DEAN The Supreme Court intervened on his behalf.

BRYNN You stopped a good woman who has successfully fostered scores of children from getting any more when you discovered she was a lesbian.

DEAN The majority of society is uncomfortable with gay foster parents.

BRYNN Actually, a recent poll says a majority of Canadians favour equal rights for gay people. They even approve of gay marriage.

DEAN Most Canadians still see marriage as a holy covenant between a man and a woman.

MARCUS Most Canadians opposed divorce until they discovered that they hated the person they were married to.

BRYNN You can't deny people rights because of their sexual orientation.

DEAN I don't believe in sexual orientation.

NASH You don't believe in evolution either do you?

DEAN No.

MARCUS How do you explain fossils, Dean?

DEAN Science lies.

NASH And religion doesn't?

MARCUS Religion lies nicely.

DEAN I believe homosexuality is a choice.

BRYNN	Not for everyone. Marcus, for example, couldn't choose to be anything but gay.
MARCUS	I was bi for a while—but not very convincingly. Like David Bowie.
NASH	I bought it.
FRITZ	But you choose to be gay?
BRYNN	Absolutely. I've lived in the straight world. I've lived in the gay world and I think the gay world's a lot more fun. Straight men get old and fat and saggy far too fast. And, unfortunately, so do the women.

AMANDA and NANCY enter with tea and dessert.

AMANDA	Tea.
FRITZ	Thank you.
NASH	Why is it always an and/or situation? Why can't people just be sexual—without labels?
MARCUS	Because we're men and men have to name everything or they don't know how to recognize it a second time.
BRYNN	Besides, too much free thinking—of any kind, makes the politicians nervous.
DEAN	Come on. It's not like I think gay people should be killed or locked up or anything like that. But I have to reflect the beliefs of my constituents.
NASH	Personally, I don't believe in marriage for anyone.
BRYNN	Then I guess this is probably a bad time to ask Marcus to marry me.
MARCUS	*(laughs)* I think so.

BRYNN removes a ring box from his pocket.

BRYNN	Too bad. I had intended to.
NANCY	Really?

BRYNN opens the box.

DEAN	Get out.

MARCUS   Are you serious?

> *BRYNN gets down on one knee and offers the ring to MARCUS.*

BRYNN   Marcus Rogers, will you marry me?

> *Pause.*

MARCUS   Um—okay.

> *BRYNN embraces MARCUS.*

BRYNN   Wonderful.

MARCUS   Maybe we could—get out of here for a bit?

BRYNN   Of course.

MARCUS   Nerves.

> *BRYNN and MARCUS exit. Pause.*

NANCY   That's so romantic.

NASH   Wow.

DEAN   They aren't serious are they?

FRITZ   I think they are.

AMANDA   Anyone for some tea?

DEAN   Sweet Jesus.

> *Lights on MARCUS and BRYNN in their room.*

MARCUS   I can't take this ring.

BRYNN   Pardon?

MARCUS   What did you want me to do—turn you down in front of a room full of people?

BRYNN   Marcus, this isn't a joke.

MARCUS   You want me to marry you?

BRYNN   Yes.

MARCUS   Why?

BRYNN	Because I love you. Because I want you to be with me—to be my partner—my best friend—for the rest of our lives. Be mine and mine alone.
MARCUS	And will you be mine and mine alone?
BRYNN	I'll try very hard.
MARCUS	You always do. You always fail.
BRYNN	No one's perfect. It doesn't affect what I feel about you.
MARCUS	No but if often affects the way I feel about myself.
BRYNN	My heart is yours.
MARCUS	But your dick is not. You're a sex addict and I'm a drug addict.
BRYNN	My point exactly. We don't have to subscribe to straight morality.
MARCUS	Then why get married at all?
BRYNN	To declare our unconventional love to the world.
MARCUS	Don't quite buy that.
BRYNN	To piss straight people off.
MARCUS	That's better.

Pause.

Where did you get the money for a ring like this?

BRYNN	I'm not without my resources.
MARCUS	I should check my email.
BRYNN	I want an answer, Marcus.

Pause.

MARCUS	All right I'll marry you.

BRYNN embraces him.

BRYNN	Thank you.
MARCUS	Now can I check my email?
BRYNN	Just a minute.

> *BRYNN slips the ring onto MARCUS's finger. They kiss.*

MARCUS   I guess we'll have to wait until we get home to do it legally.

BRYNN   No. Let's do it here.

MARCUS   Is it legal here?

BRYNN   I hope not.

> *They kiss again.*

Now you can check the bloody email.

> *Lights rise on the living room. NANCY is watching the television, flicking the channels with the remote.*

NANCY   Amanda?

> *AMANDA enters.*

AMANDA   Yes?

NANCY   Something's wrong with your TV.

AMANDA   Really?

NANCY   I can only get five channels.

AMANDA   Yes.

NANCY   Don't you have cable or satellite or something?

AMANDA   No.

NANCY   At least you have a DVD player.

AMANDA   I'm not one for technology but Keith quite liked it. He said the Internet would create a truly united world.

NANCY   Yeah like that's happened. Old people can be real eccentric huh?

AMANDA   Forty-five isn't exactly old.

NANCY   Halfway to dead. How old are you?

AMANDA   Twenty-five next month.

NANCY   Nineteen. We could almost be sisters.

AMANDA   Almost.

NANCY   You find that strange?

AMANDA   A bit. You?

NANCY   Like totally.

                        Pause.

            Any good bars or anything like that in Manchester?

AMANDA   You could go down to Deansgate.

NANCY   Are there really big horribly overpriced clubs full of
            drunken, horny, marginally attractive men who'll grope
            my butt and puke on my shoes while they're talking to me?

AMANDA   Of course. Stupidly long queues too.

NANCY   Perfect. You wanna come?

AMANDA   I don't think I should leave this lot on their own.

NANCY   They'll cope.

                        Short pause.

AMANDA   Okay.

                        *There is a sudden, loud, dramatic scream off
                        (MARCUS).*

NANCY   Jesus.

AMANDA   What was that?

                        *Lights rise on the bedroom. MARCUS is sitting
                        in front of the computer banging his head on the
                        tabletop. BRYNN is behind him.*

MARCUS   Oh God! Oh God!

BRYNN   Marcus, you really shouldn't scream like that.

MARCUS   It's over. It's all over.

BRYNN   You always say that.

MARCUS   No this time it's really all over.

                        NASH enters.

NASH   What's wrong?

BRYNN	The reviews have come out.
NASH	Oh. No.

DEAN enters.

DEAN	Marcus?
NASH	It's okay.

FRITZ enters.

FRITZ	Anything I can help with?
BRYNN	No really. He's just—upset.
MARCUS	It's all over!

NANCY and AMANDA enter.

NANCY	Someone get killed?
BRYNN	It's nothing.
MARCUS	Don't say that! Don't you dare say that! It might be nothing to you but it is everything to me.
NANCY	Okay well we don't really know anything about this stuff so Amanda and I are going out kay bye.
MARCUS	God!

NANCY and AMANDA exit.

DEAN	Were they all bad?
MARCUS	Toxic. Venomous. Cruel.
NASH	I'm sorry.
MARCUS	My label's gonna drop me. This is the last album in my contract.
FRITZ	They're only opinions.
MARCUS	Opinions that affect sales in a major fashion. Jesus. I'm a one-hit wonder who never lived up to his potential. I can't tell you how much I thought this would never happen to me.
BRYNN	It'll be okay. Your fans—
MARCUS	After thirty they're not fans they're patrons.

DEAN	At least you've got your health.
MARCUS	I'm HIV-positive, Dean.
DEAN	Yes. Right. Well. At least no one's suing you.
MARCUS	Thanks that really helps.
FRITZ	You shouldn't take them so seriously.
MARCUS	You don't know me well enough to console me.
BRYNN	Marcus, don't be so unpleasant.
MARCUS	Shut up!
DEAN	Maybe we should just leave you fellows alone for a while.
MARCUS	Yeah.
BRYNN	Thanks.
NASH	If you need anything just knock.

FRITZ, NASH, and DEAN exit. Long pause.

BRYNN	It's not the end of the world.
MARCUS	Six flops in a row, Brynn. Each one considerably less successful than the album before it. I'm not stupid. I know what this means. I'm finished as a pop star.
BRYNN	We're getting married. It won't matter.

Pause. MARCUS takes the ring off of his finger.

MARCUS	I don't think I'm the kind of wife you're looking for.

MARCUS tosses BRYNN the ring.

BRYNN	Marcus…?

MARCUS exits. Lights rise on NASH, DEAN and FRITZ in the living room, drinking around the coffin.

DEAN	That was dramatic.
NASH	Dean, you wouldn't understand.
DEAN	I get bad press all the time.

NASH	I've been lucky in a weird way. I never had the huge success Keith and Marcus had.
FRITZ	You're very well-known.
NASH	Among the art film set. I've made a marginally good living.
DEAN	You did win a Genie for best director.
FRITZ	A what?
NASH	Exactly. I love making movies—the process—but I never really cared about fame. Once the movie opens, I'm basically over it.
FRITZ	If it's any consolation I'd kill to have your modest success. I've always wanted to express myself instead of always—
NASH	What?
FRITZ	Writing what other people tell me to.
NASH	If you've seen my work you must be quite a dedicated filmgoer. Particularly in Cincinnati. Another drink?
FRITZ	Thanks. I love movies. I always have.
NASH	Who's your favourite director?
FRITZ	Martin Scorsese.
NASH	Interesting.
FRITZ	Yours?
NASH	Fellini.
DEAN	I don't see movies much anymore.
FRITZ	I would've guessed Fellini.
DEAN	Kelly says even the Disney ones seem dirty underneath.
NASH	Who's your favourite DOP?
FRITZ	Greg Tolland. You?
NASH	Svend Nykvist.
DEAN	We liked the one about the talking bird.
NASH	Editor?

FRITZ Ula Ryghe.

NASH *Persona.* Very good.

FRITZ Bergman is unparalleled.

NASH You're no financial writer.

FRITZ What?

NASH You're not the type.

FRITZ I write a stocks column for *The Cincinnati Post.*

DEAN You're being paranoid, Nash.

NASH Was Keith circumcised?

Short pause.

FRITZ Yes.

Short pause.

NASH Promise me that anything that happens this weekend—you won't write about it.

FRITZ You have my word.

NASH Why do I find it so hard to trust you?

FRITZ Because lack of trust is the defining trait of your generation.

FRITZ exits quickly.

DEAN What's gotten into you?

NASH There's something about her—

DEAN At least she's not discussing marrying someone of the same sex.

NASH That really pushes your buttons doesn't it?

DEAN I don't think—I—I don't know how to react to it.

NASH I find that hard to believe. You seem to have an opinion on everything these days.

DEAN I'm a politician.

NASH	Don't you ever worry that Marcus or I might blab about some of your—misadventures in university? You weren't as devout then.
DEAN	No.
NASH	You're very trusting.
DEAN	None of us has ever betrayed the others, Nash. Not in that way. I doubt either you or Marcus will start now.
NASH	You're probably right.

Short pause.

DEAN	You look great. You've lost weight.
NASH	You're not so bad yourself.
DEAN	Your skin is still wonderful.
NASH	Are you flirting with me?
DEAN	I'm a married man.
NASH	So you were charming me.
DEAN	Why don't you have another movie in the works?
NASH	I'm tired of being in control, Dean. All those people waiting around for me—the responsibility. It's very lonely being in control.
DEAN	I know.
NASH	Guess I'm on a sort of mid-life sabbatical. I always had my daughter to think about. Now she's grown up and I don't have to think about her so much but I suddenly find myself not knowing what else to think about.
DEAN	Maybe you need to do something else for a while.
NASH	Besides lie in bed and cry?
DEAN	Have you tried Prozac or Zoloft or any of these new antidepressants? They're very effective.
NASH	I'm avoiding all substances these days.
DEAN	Kelly was on them for a while and they seemed to help her a lot.

NASH   Why?

DEAN   Because they're effective seratonin enhancers—

NASH   No—why was Kelly on antidepressants?

DEAN   Oh she was—we had some trouble.

NASH   What was the problem?

DEAN   I was impotent for a period of time.

NASH   I'm told it happens to most men around your age.

DEAN   Yes.

Pause.

After we finished college—I used to fantasize about you a lot.

NASH   Sexually?

DEAN   I'd think about what being married to you would be like. We had many long, imaginary conversations over breakfast.

NASH   That's sweet.

DEAN   I'm sorry for what happened—

NASH   It happened.

DEAN   We were so young—

NASH   I know. And I had the bad form to get pregnant.

DEAN   I—it never occurred to me you'd slept with any of us more than that—one time.

NASH   We all thought we had our own special relationship with Keith that the others didn't share.

DEAN   We were a family until that moment.

NASH   Nothing like kids to ruin a family.

DEAN   We've all got other families now.

NASH   What was your special relationship with Keith?

Pause.

DEAN   He didn't judge me.

NASH	When did you see him last?
DEAN	Years ago. We spoke on the phone from time to time. Wrote letters. He never really accepted my—conversion.
NASH	I'm not sure any of us did.
DEAN	It helped, Nash. It gave me rules—structure. Choices became less confusing. It made things—
NASH	Easier?
DEAN	In a way. Harder in a way too. But it was better.
NASH	Was?
DEAN	Even the strongest faith goes through periods of crisis. God isn't always—immediately accessible.
NASH	Are you okay?
DEAN	Sure. Why didn't you marry?
NASH	I come from a long line of women who do well without husbands. I never really learned how to trust men. None of them ever hung around long enough for me to figure them out. Thanks, Mom. Really.
DEAN	How is your mother?
NASH	Dead.
DEAN	I'm sorry.
NASH	I hadn't been back to Edmonton in years. No one found her for about a week. Her poor cat had to eat one of her arms to stay alive.
DEAN	That's horrifying.
NASH	I think we're all destined to die alone and be eaten by our house pets.
DEAN	That's one argument for marriage.
NASH	One of you still dies alone.

Short pause.

DEAN	What happened to the cat?

NASH	You have to put them down once they've tasted human flesh.
DEAN	You're kidding.
NASH	Yes. I have no idea what happened to the cat.
DEAN	I could never tell with you.
NASH	And your parents?
DEAN	Dad passed away a few years ago. Heart attack. Mom has Alzheimer's. They keep her in a very nice place with a lot of other old people in diapers.
NASH	It's scary when all the grown-ups are dying.
DEAN	I hate sex.

> *Pause.*

I don't understand how an activity that involves only two people almost always leaves one or both of them feeling cheated.

NASH	I've had periods in my life when I've hated sex. I think everyone has.
DEAN	But it's different for you. You don't have balls.
NASH	Pardon?
DEAN	It's our balls that get men in trouble. It always has been. The balls are to blame.
NASH	I don't think the balls are much good without the brain.
DEAN	Oh you don't know the balls. The balls are—relentless. Inexorable.
NASH	You know, I came down here thinking I might come on to you—see if you could be led astray—but you're kinda freaking me out and I don't find it very stimulating.

> *Pause.*

DEAN	I need to pray.
NASH	Yes.

*NASH exits. DEAN leans on the coffin and takes
a series of deep breaths before he kneels and begins to
pray. Lights rise on MARCUS, lying on the bed,
looking dramatically desolate. There is a knock at the
door. MARCUS does not respond. The door opens
and FRITZ looks in.*

FRITZ   Critics are often proved wrong by history.

MARCUS   I can't put history in my bank trout—uh—account.

FRITZ   Have you taken something?

MARCUS   Halcyon. Halcyon's illegal now but I got a really really big prescription in the eighties when I was rich.

FRITZ   If it's any consolation I can't wait to buy the CD.

MARCUS   It's my happy album. It's filled with joy and laughter and capricious playful flourishes. I was sure there'd be a big hit—dance remix—video—but now—nothing.

FRITZ   Can I get you anything?

MARCUS   A time machine please. A time machine that'll take me back to 1986 and allow me to confront my younger self and say don't be such an asshole! Don't act like you know everything, don't date actors and don't spend all your money on drugs and gold jewellery and pretend friends and priceless antique Barbie dolls.

FRITZ   I'm sure you'll get by.

MARCUS   But I don't want to get by! I want to be rich and have four different residences and a retinue like I'm supposed to.

FRITZ   There's always Vegas.

Pause.

MARCUS   Okay now I hate you.

FRITZ   A lot of people have done very well with that sort of a come-back.

MARCUS   Are you here to try to force me to murder you?

FRITZ   You have other albums in you.

MARCUS   I'm not so sure.

FRITZ	Come on.
MARCUS	It's not the same when you're in your forties as it is when you're in your twenties or even your thirties. The edge is dulled. I don't feel things as keenly.
FRITZ	Isn't that what your critics are saying?

Pause.

MARCUS	Is Fritz your real name?

Short pause.

FRITZ	It's the name I like to be known by.
MARCUS	So it isn't your real name.
FRITZ	It's what I like to be called.
MARCUS	What are you hiding?
FRITZ	Just my unbridled admiration for you.
MARCUS	You're good.
FRITZ	I know.

FRITZ exits. A light on the living room. BRYNN, NANCY and AMANDA enter.

BRYNN	I do love English beer.
NANCY	Kinda like snot with yeast.
BRYNN	You have such a way with words.
AMANDA	Anyone for another drink?
BRYNN	Sure.
NANCY	Why not?

AMANDA gets drinks.

BRYNN	Amanda, you haven't had a real drink all night.
AMANDA	I'm not much of a drinker. How lucky we should bump into you at the bar.
BRYNN	Manchester's bigger than I remember but smaller than I thought.

AMANDA   You've been in Canada too long.

BRYNN   It's an interesting country. You should visit sometime.

AMANDA   Too far—too cold.

BRYNN   Bloody freezing. But beautiful. Everyone says Canadians are friendly but what they are is courteous. Courteous and friendly are very different things.

NANCY   We're the British without the reserve and the Americans without the insincerity.

AMANDA   And you don't live in igloos?

NANCY   Yeah—but we get tents in the summer.

AMANDA   I should go.

NANCY   No.

BRYNN   Really. You really must tell us more about yourself. You seem a fascinating creature.

AMANDA   Don't patronize me.

NANCY   So were you doing the great and mighty Keith or what?

AMANDA   I don't see that that's any of your business.

NANCY   You were doing him.

AMANDA   We were—partners.

BRYNN   Business partners—dance partners—sexual partners—be specific.

AMANDA   Is he less of a partner if we weren't having sex?

NANCY   No. I'm just nosey and everyone else is too afraid to ask.

AMANDA   Honestly—between the three of us only—Keith drank a bottle of bourbon and smoked two packets of cigarettes a day. He wasn't a particularly—amorous man.

NANCY   So never?

AMANDA   Twice. Both times in the morning before he'd peed. I loved his voice. And his mind. He taught me so many things— how to talk. To think. He liked to—play with my brain. Ask me questions. Present problems. Propose conundrums.

He'd talk me in circles—argue against my conclusions—
show me where the logic fell apart—frankly it was better
than any sex I've ever had.

BRYNN   I could change that.

AMANDA   Oh do come on.

BRYNN   Sorry—things like that slip out sometimes.

AMANDA   I'm not a washed-up pop star waiting for people to tell him
what he wants to hear.

BRYNN   He's not washed-up.

AMANDA   Sorry. That was a stupid thing to say.

NANCY   I'm a virgin.

> *Pause.*

AMANDA   Canadians have a very odd sense of timing.

NANCY   I said that because everyone here seems to have had sex
with everyone else here and it's kinda wierding me out.

BRYNN   I haven't had sex with either of you.

NANCY   You're gay.

BRYNN   I thought I was bi.

NANCY   You're whatever makes you the least threatening at the
moment. I need another drink.

AMANDA   Help yourself.

NANCY   You marrying Marcus or what?

BRYNN   I'd rather not discuss that right now.

NANCY   Tough. I wanna know about it—don't you Amanda?

AMANDA   Yes. I know a Wiccan priestess who performs same-sex
marriages.

NANCY   They're not legal yet.

AMANDA   No but they are highly symbolic.

BRYNN   I'd like to have it done as soon as possible.

AMANDA   I'll call her in the morning.

NANCY	How is it you know a Wiccan priestess?
AMANDA	I know a great many interesting people. Why do you think I wouldn't?
NANCY	Relax. Nothing personal.

Pause.

NANCY	So Brynn—are you HIV positive too?
BRYNN	Negative.
AMANDA	Isn't that difficult with a positive partner?
BRYNN	No. I've never had sex without a condom. Amanda, you're an attractive girl. I can't believe Keith wasn't more attentive.
AMANDA	I never should have told you that.
BRYNN	It was a compliment.

AMANDA begins to move off.

NANCY	Where're you going?
AMANDA	I'm tired.
BRYNN	Amanda?
AMANDA	Yes?
BRYNN	What kind of—agreement did you have with Keith?
AMANDA	We'll find out tomorrow when we read the will.
NANCY	There's a will?
AMANDA	Of course.
BRYNN	He never discussed it with you?
AMANDA	No.
BRYNN	He must be worth a fortune.
AMANDA	I suspect so.
NANCY	Really?
AMANDA	Perhaps Nancy will get everything.
NANCY	No way.

AMANDA   You never know.

               AMANDA exits.

NANCY   When I got here I only understood about every third word she said—but I'm getting quite good at it now. She hates me right?

BRYNN   I'm sure she doesn't.

NANCY   You didn't get a hate vibe?

BRYNN   No but I'm not always in tune with these things. I find getting involved in other people's intimate lives rather—embarrassing.

NANCY   Your parents didn't hug and kiss you much when you were a kid did they?

BRYNN   I had a nanny who kissed me once.

NANCY   I've been getting a vibe from you.

BRYNN   What sort of a vibe?

NANCY   A sexual vibe.

BRYNN   Don't take it personally.

NANCY   I might want to take it personally.

BRYNN   Are you coming on to me?

NANCY   Got a problem with that?

BRYNN   Are you drunk?

NANCY   Not that drunk.

               BRYNN moves to NANCY and kisses her deeply.

BRYNN   What do you think?

NANCY   I think we should sneak up to my room very, very quietly.

               BRYNN sweeps NANCY up in her arms and carries her out of the room like a bride. Lights rise on FRITZ in her bedroom working on her laptop. There is a knock at her door. She turns off the laptop and closes it. DEAN enters.

DEAN	Ula Ryghe?! No financial writer is going to know who someone named Ula Ryghe is.
FRITZ	I admit that was a bit foolish. But—I find it so hard to pretend not to know things. And she's so talented. It's slightly intimidating.
DEAN	I can't afford to have anything go wrong.
FRITZ	What do you plan to tell your wife when you get home?

Pause.

DEAN	I've talked to her about it. In a general way.
FRITZ	So you think you can do this without her knowing and she'll just accept your choice?
DEAN	Choice?! If I had a choice we never would have met on the Internet. If I had a choice things wouldn't've worked out with the amazing precision with which they've worked out. I have no choice. I—I still can't believe this is really happening.
FRITZ	I understand your confusion. But you have to trust me.
DEAN	Okay.
FRITZ	Now, get out of here before your friends start to get suspicious.
DEAN	Right.

Short pause.

How did you know Keith was circumcised?

Short pause.

FRITZ	Lucky guess.

FRITZ exits to the bathroom. DEAN exits to the corridor. Lights change as NASH moves to the bed from the bathroom. There is a knock at the door.

NASH	Hello?

MARCUS enters.

MARCUS	Pyjama party?

NASH   Sure.

    MARCUS climbs into bed with NASH.

NASH   How are you feeling?

MARCUS   Like the whole world's seen me naked and laughed at my dick.

NASH   You're still Marcus. You're special.

MARCUS   I was special until I came out. After that I was just gay.

NASH   You've always been you.

MARCUS   It's not working. It hasn't for a long time. It's so weird. All my life I worked to be a famous pop star—

NASH   And you did it.

MARCUS   For a minute in 1986.

NASH   For a good couple of years, buddy.

MARCUS   I never appreciated it, Nash. Not once. And I'm not gonna get a second chance. I can feel it. It's over. I was a shitty punk rocker. I was a shitty rebel. I let them trap me with their promises of easy money. God is punishing me.

NASH   I have cancer.

    Long pause. MARCUS moves closer to NASH and takes her hand.

    I found a lump in my breast about two weeks ago. The day we left to fly here the oncologist's office called. They want me to come in for a consultation. Early next week.

MARCUS   Nash.

NASH   I'm hoping we caught it early.

MARCUS   Don't assume anything until you know for sure.

NASH   I haven't told anyone.

MARCUS   Not even Nancy?

NASH   No.

MARCUS   Why not?

NASH   My mother died of cancer—my aunt just had a double
            mastectomy. You think I should ruin her future before it's
            begun?

MARCUS   But will you tell her?

NASH   Yes. When the time is right.

MARCUS   They're going to invent sliding sidewalks, robot maids and
            the cure for cancer before Nancy turns thirty.

NASH   I'm scared.

MARCUS   I know.

NASH   Everything—everything just changed. It's all a struggle now.

MARCUS   I know.

NASH   I could die.

MARCUS   I know.

NASH   Stop saying that.

MARCUS   But I do know, Nash. I know about unwelcome strangers
            taking up residence in your body. I know about the
            possibility of death. I do know.

NASH   I know.

MARCUS   I know.

                        They kiss.

NASH   Any advice?

MARCUS   Pray.

NASH   I've never known you to be religious.

MARCUS   You don't have to be religious to pray, darling.

NASH   Does it work?

MARCUS   I don't think prayer can get rid of your cancer—any more
            than it can take this virus out of my system. But it can
            help us deal with it. And I'm living proof that miracles
            do happen.

NASH   Miracles?

MARCUS	I was dead, honey. I was in the ER in an isolation tank with a virus racing through my brain that would have killed me within days if someone hadn't decided to try a new combination of drugs they were just beginning to use. Within three months it was like I was never sick. Everyone I knew is dead. I lived. It wasn't supposed to happen.
NASH	I'm just—I'm scared they're going to cut me.
MARCUS	They cut us all eventually.
NASH	I'm already starting to feel like an unattractive middle-aged woman. The thought of losing my breasts—
MARCUS	You don't direct films with your breasts.
NASH	If I'd eaten more vegetables—quit drinking sooner—exercised more—
MARCUS	Hadn't done ecstasy at the circuit party—hadn't paid for that porn star in New York—hadn't drunk so much in Berlin—hadn't had a life. Don't go there, girl.
NASH	Feeling any better about the reviews?
MARCUS	Who cares now?
NASH	I can feel it in my body. Something's—not right.
MARCUS	You're not unattractive, Nash.
NASH	Thanks.
MARCUS	You look better than you ever have.
NASH	I'll accept that as a compliment.

They have snuggled very close by this point.

You've always been a star.

MARCUS	You've always been a gorgeous woman.
NASH	You've stayed in shape.
MARCUS	You too.

Pause.

NASH	Are you feeling me up?
MARCUS	No.

NASH   Yes.

MARCUS   Okay.

> *Pause.*

Do you mind?

NASH   Not really.

MARCUS   Want to neck?

NASH   Okay.

> *They neck, getting turned on.*

NASH   Marcus—?

MARCUS   Shhh.

> *They kiss again and laugh quietly. Lights slowly fade to black.*

Act Two

> *Lights rise on NASH's bed. NASH is sleeping.*
> *Someone unseen is bundled under the covers next*
> *to her. NASH wakes. Nervously, she pulls back the*
> *covers. NANCY smiles up at her mother.*

NANCY   Hey.

NASH   What time did you come in?

NANCY   I don't know. Late. Who did you think was in bed with you?

NASH   Nothing no one.

> *NASH gets out of bed.*

NANCY   I've got such a hangover. What did you do?

NASH   Oh, just visited with Dean and Marcus you know. You haven't gotten in bed with me for years.

NANCY   There's something I should maybe tell you.

NASH   No there's something I have to tell you.

NANCY   What?

NASH   And when I tell you this please try to keep your emotions in control. It'll be hard but try.

NANCY   What?

NASH   I have—

NANCY   You're being theatrical mother.

> *Short pause.*

NASH   I had sex with Marcus last night.

> *Long pause.*

NASH   We had safe sex.

NANCY   That is so gross.

NASH   Because he's gay?

NANCY   Because you're my mother. Do you have to tell me everything?

NASH	I thought we were friends.
NANCY	I'm your daughter.

NANCY gets out of bed.

NASH	I don't know how it happened.
NANCY	Was it—okay?
NASH	Yes. Very okay. I'd prefer it if you didn't say anything. I don't know how he handles these things with Brynn—and it was—nothing really—old friends getting reacquainted.
NANCY	You have sex to get reacquainted? Don't worry, I'll keep my mouth shut.
NASH	What was it you wanted to tell me?
NANCY	Nothing.

NASH and NANCY exit the bedroom. Lights change on the bedroom. The shower is heard in the bathroom. MARCUS is heard speaking to BRYNN in the bathroom.

MARCUS	What time did you get in?
BRYNN	I don't remember. Late.
MARCUS	Did you have fun?

Sound of the toilet flushing.

BRYNN	What?
MARCUS	Did you have fun?!
BRYNN	Yes. I ran into Nancy and Amanda.

MARCUS enters from the bathroom in his underwear. He dresses. Sound of the shower being turned off.

You were dead to the world when I got in. Didn't even move when I kissed you goodnight.

MARCUS	I was exhausted.
BRYNN	What's on the agenda for today?
MARCUS	Wanna go see where they film "Coronation Street"?

BRYNN   They don't do that anymore.

MARCUS   We could shop.

BRYNN   That might not be such a great idea at the moment.

> *BRYNN enters from the bathroom, wearing his underwear and towelling his hair. He dresses.*

MARCUS   Why not?

BRYNN   I did a quick money check on-line. We're broke shortly.

> *BRYNN makes the bed.*

MARCUS   I had sex with Nash last night.

> *Pause.*

Are you mad?

BRYNN   I don't—no—stunned. I'd hate to think you've started sleeping with women in order to avoid making a commitment to me.

MARCUS   It's not that simple.

BRYNN   Was it good?

MARCUS   I was great.

BRYNN   That's hot.

MARCUS   Aren't you a bit jealous?

BRYNN   Why should I be?

MARCUS   Because I slept with someone else.

BRYNN   Marcus, we're men. I know it doesn't mean anything.

MARCUS   But it did mean something.

BRYNN   What did it mean?

MARCUS   Something.

BRYNN   I don't feel seriously threatened by the possibility you might leave me for Nash, Marcus.

MARCUS   Maybe you should.

BRYNN   Really?

Pause.

MARCUS   I don't know.

        BRYNN moves to MARCUS and touches him.

BRYNN   It just makes you more attractive to me.

MARCUS   You are unbelievable.

BRYNN   Want a bit of the pointy-oink?

        BRYNN kisses MARCUS passionately.

MARCUS   Okay.

BRYNN   Amanda knows a Wiccan priestess who can marry us.

MARCUS   Great.

BRYNN   And then I think we're going to have to discuss children.

MARCUS   We have no place to store children. Besides I'm too poor now.

        MARCUS begins to kiss BRYNN's chest.

BRYNN   Poor people have families.

MARCUS   Yeah, but it's boring. Trust me. Now lie down.

BRYNN   Whatever you say.

        Lights rise on the dining room. FRITZ is at the table working on her laptop. AMANDA enters from the kitchen with coffee, which she gives to FRITZ.

AMANDA   Is it hard? Writing every day like that?

FRITZ   Sometimes it's the easiest thing in the world and other times it's like torture.

AMANDA   Keith encouraged me to write. He said anyone could do it.

FRITZ   True. But not everyone can write things other people want to read. You should write about your time with Keith. Now that would sell.

AMANDA   I'd never do that.

FRITZ   Never say never.

AMANDA   It wouldn't seem right.

FRITZ	You can't hurt dead people.

DEAN enters.

DEAN	Good morning.
FRITZ	Good morning.
DEAN	Did you ladies sleep all right?
FRITZ	Like the dead. But I always do.
DEAN	I had nightmares.
FRITZ	I don't dream. Never have.
AMANDA	Would you like tea or coffee?
DEAN	Coffee. Please.

AMANDA exits.

FRITZ	Nightmares?
DEAN	I have—
FRITZ	Doubts.
DEAN	The ramifications—
FRITZ	What'll happen if you back out now?
DEAN	I'll go back to my wife and family exactly as I left them. Everything will be as it always was.
FRITZ	You know that's not true.
DEAN	It is—

AMANDA enters with coffee.

AMANDA	Everything okay?
DEAN	Fine.
AMANDA	I have to pop over to Keith's solicitors and pick up the will.
FRITZ	Of course there would be a will.
DEAN	Interesting.
AMANDA	There's toast and Marmite in the kitchen.

AMANDA exits.

DEAN   What's Marmite?

FRITZ   Yet another vile thing the English love to eat. There are times when we all have to put thoughts of consequence behind us and just do what we have to.

DEAN   I know.

NASH enters.

NASH   It's always so scary to enter a room where two people are whispering.

DEAN   I know how you artistic types like to sleep late.

NASH   I've been a morning person ever since I stopped dropping acid.

FRITZ   LSD? Really? I've never done any drugs.

NASH   You poor suckers who were kids in the eighties. You missed everything. No wonder you're all so cynical. Why do you look so down, Dean?

DEAN   Just thinking. Sorry.

FRITZ   Amanda left tea and breakfast in the kitchen.

NASH   Thanks.

NASH exits.

DEAN   I have a career to think of.

FRITZ   Oh please. If your career were so important you wouldn't be here at all.

DEAN   I don't like it when you talk to me like that.

FRITZ   I don't care.

NASH enters with coffee and a scone.

NASH   That girl's been an angel. You know this can't be easy for her.

FRITZ   I feel the urge to shop. Excuse me.

FRITZ exits.

NASH	They're a different generation. You just know they'll have no trouble accepting euthanasia as a viable alternative to long-term care. Have you seen Marcus yet?
DEAN	I passed his room on my way down. They sounded—busy.
NASH	Really?
DEAN	Very.
NASH	Huh.

BRYNN enters.

BRYNN	Good morning.
DEAN	Hello.
NASH	Are you sweating?
BRYNN	Glowing. How was your night?
NASH	Eventful.
BRYNN	I heard.
DEAN	Where's Marcus?
BRYNN	Showering. Have you seen Amanda?
DEAN	She just left.
BRYNN	Damn. Where's Nancy?
NASH	I think the jet lag's finally hit her.
BRYNN	She's hard to resist. Bright and sassy. It's an unbeatable combination.
DEAN	Are you sure you're gay?

MARCUS enters.

MARCUS	It's so hard to tell with British men.
NASH	They all seem gay.
MARCUS	Oddly—so do their fathers.
DEAN	You're looking fit, Marcus.
MARCUS	Feeling good. Morning, Nash.
NASH	Morning, buddy.

MARCUS   Where's the journalist?

DEAN   She's a financial writer. She went shopping.

MARCUS   Does anyone feel like attending a wedding today?

DEAN   Marcus, I think it's only fair to warn you that if you insist on going through with this thing I may have to leave.

          Pause.

MARCUS   Nash, will you join me as I assemble my trousseau?

NASH   Okay, but you know I have no taste in men's clothes.

MARCUS   Who said anything about men's clothes?

DEAN   No.

MARCUS   Maybe.

          MARCUS and NASH exit. Lights rise on the bedroom. NANCY is working on her laptop. There is a knock at her door.

NANCY   Hi.

BRYNN   Busy?

NANCY   Just answering email.

          BRYNN enters.

BRYNN   How's the hangover?

NANCY   Fading but I do feel like my eyeballs have been blow-torched.

BRYNN   I wanted to make sure everything's—okay.

NANCY   I'm fine. Did Marcus tell you about—?

BRYNN   Yes. You're going to have to tell Nash aren't you?

NANCY   Sure. And you're gonna have to tell Marcus.

BRYNN   Marcus doesn't really like to know about the other people I sleep with. Unless it's important in some way.

NANCY   This is important in some way.

BRYNN   I'm quite accustomed to recreational sex. It doesn't have to mean anything.

NANCY   Hopefully, it means you're at least attracted to the person.

BRYNN   Yes. That's nice when it happens.

NANCY   I will have to tell my mother. She's never lied to me.

BRYNN   So you must never lie to her.

NANCY   Isn't it like so unfair for a parent to do that?

BRYNN   Wildly selfish. I don't suppose you could hold it off until tomorrow. I don't want to set Marcus off again.

NANCY   It'll be hard. It's like she can read my mind sometimes.

BRYNN   Do try.

NANCY   I'll do my best.

        Pause.

BRYNN   Was I okay?

NANCY   You know you were. It was—better than I'd been led to believe. Is that how you make love to Marcus?

        Quick pause.

BRYNN   It's—different with each person.

NANCY   You really do love him.

BRYNN   Yes. I always have. From the first time I ever heard him sing. That voice. Of course he had no idea I was a fan when I met him. Hates that sort of thing.

NANCY   So I was what? A diversion? A conquest?

BRYNN   I prefer to think of you as a piece in a beautiful mosaic that I've been constructing all of my life without really knowing what it is.

NANCY   Oh please.

BRYNN   Really. And it will be finished someday too. Then I'll be able to stand back and view the entire thing and say, "That's what that meant."

NANCY   If you weren't so cheesy I could really like you.

BRYNN   Can we be friends?

NANCY	I should hope so.
BRYNN	Good.
NANCY	Can I tell you something in strict confidence?
BRYNN	Sure.
NANCY	I have a crush on Amanda.
BRYNN	Really?
NANCY	I feel funny when she walks into a room. I spend a lot more time brushing my teeth. What's wrong with me?
BRYNN	Absolutely nothing. Although it could be a phase.
NANCY	I feel weird I told you that. Could you tell me something secret and personal so I don't feel so weird?
BRYNN	Well—
NANCY	Anything. I feel really weird.
BRYNN	I'm rich.
NANCY	You're not like nobility or something like that are you?
BRYNN	No just an upper middle-class boy who had a very ambitious great-grandfather. Nobody in Canada knows. Not even Marcus.
NANCY	Why are you so hung up about it?
BRYNN	It's not something I've earned. I've watched it ruin my family. My father's never worked a day in his life and is slowly drinking himself to death. My mother's a ghost with a credit card. My brother—don't get me started—so when I immigrated to Canada I just—dropped it. Along with most everything else in my past.
NANCY	So I'm a closet bisexual lesbian and you're a closet gay-by-choice heiress.
BRYNN	Nancy, this is all strictly *entre nous*.
NANCY	*No problemo por favor.*
BRYNN	The weekend's already going to be full of enough unexpected surprises.

NANCY   What does that mean?

BRYNN   Nothing. Really.

> NASH enters.

NASH   Sweetie, do you have the—

> NASH sees BRYNN and stops abruptly.

Sorry. I thought you'd be alone.

BRYNN   We're sharing hangover remedies.

NASH   Not drinking works wonderfully. I need the adaptor.

NANCY   Just take it off of my computer.

BRYNN   Is Marcus back as well?

NASH   No. I just couldn't bear to watch him try on any more clothes.

BRYNN   How was he paying?

NASH   With a charge card.

BRYNN   That could be tragic. Any sign of Amanda?

NASH   I haven't seen her.

BRYNN   Right. Excuse me.

> BRYNN exits.

NASH   Have you decided to sleep with him or have you already slept with him?

NANCY   What?

NASH   I'm not stupid, Nancy. You could practically choke on the pheromones when I walked into this room.

NANCY   Mother—

NASH   I'd prefer it if you discovered your burgeoning whateverness with people outside of my circle of friends. Things here are complicated enough.

NANCY   All I've ever done is complicate things between you and your friends.

NASH   You know that's not what I'm saying.

NANCY   I didn't even want to come. You made me.

NASH   I did not make you—

NANCY   You did. You said it would be good for both of us. I didn't
           realize that meant good for me as long as I keep my mouth
           shut and stay out of the way.

NASH   Now you're being theatrical.

NANCY   I always get theatrical when you're directing me.

NASH   I'm not directing you.

NANCY   Yes you are.

                    Pause.

NASH   I love you, Nancy. I think you've grown up into a strong,
           unique woman. I know I didn't give you everything other
           kids got but I gave you everything I had.

NANCY   You're acting like one of those mothers on TV who just
           found out she has a brain tumour.

NASH   Shut up and hug me.

NANCY   Ick.

                    *They embrace. Lights rise on the living area. DEAN
                    is there. MARCUS enters with bags and sets them on
                    the coffin. DEAN stands.*

DEAN   Excuse me—

                    DEAN tries to exit. MARCUS steps in front of him.

MARCUS   Do you remember when you called me to tell me you and
           Kelly were getting married? I was happy for you, Dean.
           Genuinely happy. Do you really think it's wrong for me to
           feel that way too?

DEAN   No. Of course not. It's just—that's not the world I live in.
           But I want everyone to be happy. And I don't want to argue
           about it, Marcus. Please.

MARCUS   We always did argue, Dean. We used to argue about music.

DEAN   Only because you hated Talking Heads.

MARCUS   Talking Heads were pretentious.

DEAN   The Cars were excellent.

MARCUS   The Cars?! Ohmigod—I bet you liked the Beatles too. You did. I remember. You liked the Beatles.

DEAN   The Beatles were the most important band in history.

MARCUS   The Monkees were better.

DEAN   Now you're really starting to make me mad.

MARCUS   Blondie had more integrity than the Beatles.

DEAN   Blondie had style. That isn't the same as integrity.

MARCUS   And nobody beats the Pretenders.

DEAN   Agreed.

MARCUS   What?

DEAN   I agree with you.

MARCUS   Really?

DEAN   We used to sit in your room and listen to "Precious" and "Brass in Pocket" over and over again on your eight-track.

MARCUS   Hey, that's right.

DEAN   We had a lot of common ground at one time.

MARCUS   That's because we were both freaks.

DEAN   I didn't wear eyeliner.

MARCUS   No but you were a political science major with an accounting minor.

                Pause.

            And you were a virgin.

DEAN   Yes. I was.

MARCUS   So was I.

DEAN   No.

MARCUS   Yeah. Nash was my first. Not exactly what I'd imagined. Keith was my second. Closer.

DEAN   Nash was my first too.

Pause.

DEAN   Marcus—I just want you to know—that I'm sorry. About your HIV status.

MARCUS   Thanks.

DEAN   I don't—I understand that judging each other and trying to force one person's idea of what's right on another person doesn't work. It doesn't work any better here than it did at The World Trade or anyplace else. I know that now and I'm sorry if I've said things in the past that have hurt you.

MARCUS   Are you okay, Dean?

Pause.

DEAN   You're not really going to wear a dress are you?

MARCUS   No. My legs are too thin.

>*FRITZ enters with large bags containing something heavy. She struggles with them. There is metal clanking from within the bags.*

FRITZ   Oh. Hello.

MARCUS   My God. What have you got in there?

FRITZ   Oh just some—pots and pans I saw and had to have.

MARCUS   Do you need a hand?

FRITZ   I'm okay!

>*FRITZ exits with bags.*

MARCUS   That's gonna make for a lot of carry-on.

DEAN   I'm sure she'll make arrangements to ship them.

MARCUS   You don't find her kinda creepy do you?

DEAN   Do you?

MARCUS   Definitely.

>*NASH enters carrying papers.*

NASH   There's a very good reason for that.

MARCUS   What?

NASH   Her name's not Fritz Harris. It's Rhonda Brown. She is from
              Cincinnati and she is a writer, but she is not a financial
              writer—she's a goddamn film critic!

MARCUS   Rhonda Brown? I knew it.

DEAN   What? No—

              NASH thrusts the papers at DEAN and MARCUS,
              who take them.

NASH   It was a nightmare locating her. I finally found a press
              gallery with pictures.

DEAN   No. It's some sort of mistake. I mean—she's so—she's so—
              she's so—nice. She's so nice and she—she knows so much.
              How could she know that much unless Keith told her?

NASH   Dean, climb offa Planet Stupid. She's a journalist.

MARCUS   It's you.

NASH   What?

MARCUS   She's stalking you. It has to be. You're the filmmaker. She's
              developed an obsession with you. She identifies with you.
              She wants to be you. Critics are all like that on the inside.
              Those who have insides.

DEAN   She's done nothing suspicious.

MARCUS   Let's kill her.

DEAN   What?

MARCUS   We could kill her and then mail pieces of her to other
              critics around the world with "You're Next" written on body
              parts in black felt pen. Let's do that. That would be fun.

DEAN   Marcus, please.

MARCUS   Okay, then let's just kick her ass outa here. Nash, since she's
              a film critic you can have the honours.

NASH   Let's search her room.

DEAN   Why do you have to search her room?

MARCUS   To see if she has any unflattering secret video footage of us
              duh.

DEAN   She has reassured us a number of times that she isn't
          writing about this weekend. Okay, she lied about what she
          does—but it's easy to understand why.

MARCUS   For you anyway.

NASH   Yes. You've been awfully understanding from the beginning.

DEAN   I'm not like you people. I don't confront anything I don't
          know with hostility.

MARCUS   Unless they're gay, black or unable to find work.

NASH   Okay boys—stop. Dean, if you think it's wrong for us to
          search her room then we won't. But I've got my eye on
          her and if she pulls anything that smells vaguely like dirty
          business I'm all over her.

DEAN   Understood.

          Pause.

          Well. I should. Go. Now.

MARCUS   Yes.

          DEAN exits.

NASH   She really did like "Another Meat Butterfly"—but she said
          "Sandalwood Woman" was self-consciously intellectual and
          pretentious. And she said "Red Tip" was anti-female.

MARCUS   That bitch! Do you think Dean'll warn her?

NASH   I think there's something going on between them.

MARCUS   I've had that feeling too.

NASH   They'll be watching us now.

MARCUS   So we get someone else to check them out.

NASH   Right.

          Short pause.

          Marcus—what sort of—fidelity agreement do you have
          with Brynn?

MARCUS   The same "don't-ask-don't-tell" kinda agreement everyone
          else has whether they know it or not—why?

NASH   He and Nancy were talking today and I got this—vibe.

MARCUS   Maybe it's just your guilty conscience.

NASH   Do you feel guilty?

MARCUS   I feel—surprised.

NASH   But if they were together when we were together—

MARCUS   That's too weird. Shut up.

              Lights rise on FRITZ's bedroom. FRITZ is working
              on her laptop. DEAN enters.

DEAN   Nash found out you're a critic.

FRITZ   How?

DEAN   The same way everyone finds out everything that's horrible.

FRITZ   The Internet.

DEAN   Yes.

FRITZ   Okay—but they don't know why I'm really here.

              FRITZ turns off her computer.

DEAN   What'll we do?

FRITZ   You're the politician. Blow smoke up their asses until
              they're distracted.

DEAN   Maybe you should move to the hotel now. I can meet you
              there tomorrow.

FRITZ   Yeah. Right. Dean, I walked in here feeling like the stupid,
              fat girl in high school being asked to hang out with all the
              cool kids. Having you here makes it pretty much perfect.
              I intend to enjoy this so I'd suggest you just relax and shut
              up until it's over.

DEAN   This isn't a game.

FRITZ   Grow up. Everything's a game.

              There is a knock at the door.

              Yes?

              NANCY is heard off.

NANCY   Can I ask you something?

FRITZ   Just a minute. *(to DEAN)* Get in the bathroom moron.

DEAN   Yes of course okay.

> *DEAN exits into the bathroom. FRITZ opens the door.*

FRITZ   Yes?

NANCY   Do you have any discs?

FRITZ   Discs?

NANCY   Computer discs.

FRITZ   I think so.

NANCY   I keep a journal on my computer and I'm worried about losing it with these weird plug-ins.

FRITZ   Here you go.

NANCY   You look kinda—pale.

FRITZ   It's the green walls.

NANCY   Okay. Thanks.

> *Pause.*

FRITZ   Yes?

NANCY   Can I ask you something personal?

FRITZ   Sure. Although I may not answer it.

NANCY   Have you had—work done?

FRITZ   Work?

NANCY   Cosmetic.

FRITZ   Oh. Yes, of course. I've had a couple procedures.

NANCY   Can I ask what they were?

FRITZ   No.

NANCY   Right.

> *NANCY exits. After a moment, DEAN enters from the bathroom.*

DEAN	That is exactly the kind of thing we cannot allow to happen.
FRITZ	Shut up.
	Pause.
DEAN	Don't talk to me—
FRITZ	Get out.
	DEAN exits. FRITZ exits to the bathroom. Lights change. NASH and NANCY enter NASH's bedroom.
NANCY	I could hear talking, but when I knocked there was no one else in the room. She looked at the bathroom door twice.
NASH	You think Dean was in there?
NANCY	Yeah.
NASH	But what would they be up to?
NANCY	Sex?
	Pause.
NASH	Honey, there's something I have to tell you—
NANCY	Actually there's something I've got to tell you.
NASH	What?
NANCY	I had sex with Brynn last night.
NASH	I knew it.
NANCY	I didn't want my first time to be with someone I was too attached to cuz what if it was disappointing?—but I didn't want some dickhead either. Brynn seemed like he'd know what he was doing. And it was time.
NASH	Has he told Marcus?
NANCY	He wants to keep it quiet until after the wedding.
NASH	How do you feel?
NANCY	Relieved. Profoundly different. Very alert. Some mothers might be shocked by all of this.

NASH   You're not going to start resenting me for not being like other mothers now are you?

NANCY   No. It's just—

NASH   What?

NANCY   I think I'm a lesbian.

        Pause.

NASH   Really?

NANCY   I don't necessarily mean a lesbian lesbian. I could be like a dilettante lesbian or an experimental lesbian or a practice lesbian or something.

NASH   I had a two-year relationship with another woman my last year of high school and my first year of university.

NANCY   Mom, we were talking about me.

NASH   I was just trying to—reassure you.

NANCY   No you weren't. You were just trying to make it all about you again.

NASH   I was trying to let you know that I don't disapprove if you are actually a lesbian.

NANCY   But I want you to disapprove!

NASH   What?

NANCY   You keep me from getting close to people.

NASH   Nancy, why are you so angry with me?

NANCY   Because you never lie to me!

        NANCY exits.

NASH   Nancy?

        NASH exits. Lights change in the bedroom. BRYNN and MARCUS enter their room.

BRYNN   A film critic? Why's she here?

MARCUS I think she's stalking Nash. Don't let on that you know.

BRYNN   My lips are sealed.

MARCUS   Nash has this crazy idea that something's going on between you and her daughter. I said it was highly unlikely but it isn't really is it—unlikely?

BRYNN   I shagged her last night.

                Pause.

MARCUS   Brynn, I learned a long time ago not to let your infidelities get to me but you know that's too close to home.

BRYNN   I also know you were having it off with her mother at the same time.

MARCUS   Only retroactively.

BRYNN   Perhaps I knew instinctually.

MARCUS   You'd just asked me to marry you.

BRYNN   And you'd just turned me down.

MARCUS   So you betrayed me.

BRYNN   You're the one who stepped completely out of character by having sex with a woman. It's—well it's threatening—it's disorienting and it's—unfair.

MARCUS   Why is it whenever you're unfaithful it always somehow turns out to be my fault?

BRYNN   It's a mistake we both made.

MARCUS   Yeah but it was my first mistake.

BRYNN   Let's leave now.

MARCUS   What?

BRYNN   Let's throw our things back into our bags and go back to the airport and wait for the next flight. Right now. Let's just walk away from this hideous weekend and these people and go home before—

MARCUS   Before what?

BRYNN   Before things get worse.

MARCUS   What do you know that I don't?

BRYNN　　　Nothing. I don't—I'm just—projecting along the established pattern.

MARCUS　　I'll leave now if we go to London. If you show me the places where you grew up. Introduce me to your oldest friends. Maybe point your family out from a discreet distance.

BRYNN puts his arms around MARCUS.

BRYNN　　　I don't care who we were or how we met or why it happened. I'm just glad to be with you. I love you, Marcus.

MARCUS　　I know.

Lights fade on the bedroom and rise on the living room. AMANDA is setting the table with a number of plates of cold food. NANCY enters, kicking the coffin angrily.

NANCY　　　All parents should be dead! Asshole!

AMANDA　　All right—enough talking around it then. You resent me for knowing your father when you didn't, don't you? Go ahead. I'm not afraid to discuss it.

Pause.

NANCY　　　When I'm in the room with you my lungs feel half their size. My skin gets red and prickly. I smile too much.

Pause.

AMANDA　　Oh.

NANCY　　　And it's wierding me out because you're my father's lover.

AMANDA　　Occasional lover. Rare really. I think he thought of me more as a daughter.

Pause.

I hated it.

NANCY　　　I'm hoping it's a phase.

Pause.

AMANDA　　Do you want to snog me?

NANCY　　　Okay.

        Pause.

        Is that like a dirty lesbian thing?

AMANDA   It means kiss me.

NANCY   You've done this before.

AMANDA   I went to an all-girls school.

NANCY   Oh right. They do that to you people over here.

AMANDA   Most girls I know learned to kiss from other girls.

        NANCY kisses AMANDA tentatively. Pause.

NANCY   Hmmm.

AMANDA   Was it what you expected?

NANCY   I'm not sure. Let's do it again. I'll be the girl this time.

AMANDA   We can both be the girl.

NANCY   Right. Cool.

        They kiss again. BRYNN enters, watching them for a moment.

BRYNN   You ladies make a charming couple.

        NANCY and AMANDA break the kiss.

AMANDA   A kiss does not a couple make.

BRYNN   It makes them a couple for a moment. Relax. Your unspoken Sapphic secret is safe with me. *(to NANCY)* I hope this isn't happening because you actually found me inadequate.

NANCY   It's an apples oranges kinda thing.

BRYNN   And do you have a preference?

NANCY   I think you're both very nice.

AMANDA   But not what you expected?

NANCY   I don't know.

BRYNN   Amanda, have you gotten hold of your Wiccan friend yet?

AMANDA   I left her a message. I think she's got a wedding in Bury today.

BRYNN   Bugger. So how soon can we see her?

AMANDA   I don't know.

BRYNN   If there's any possible way that Marcus and I can be married before the will is read—

AMANDA   I'm afraid you're a bit late.

NASH and MARCUS enter.

MARCUS   Time to read the will.

NASH   It's quite exciting.

MARCUS   Hopefully he left us all money. Lots and lots of money.

DEAN enters.

DEAN   Evening.

AMANDA   I've laid out an array of cold meats and cheeses. Please help yourselves.

NASH   It's like a party.

BRYNN   A cold meat party.

NASH   Cold meat party?

BRYNN   It's old underworld slang for a funeral.

NANCY   In what universe?

NASH   Are you still angry with me?

NANCY   Yes.

NASH   Why?

NANCY   Because I don't think I'm a lesbian!

FRITZ enters.

FRITZ   What is it about the reading of a person's last will and testament that makes the occasion so festive?

MARCUS   Uh—it's their last will and testament.

AMANDA   Isn't anyone going to eat?

NASH   Perhaps we could just get the will out of the way, dear.

BRYNN   Shouldn't the lawyer be doing this? I don't think we can do this without a lawyer.

AMANDA   Keith insisted this document is to be read privately.

BRYNN   Wouldn't we all rather do the wedding first then the will? That seems the proper thing to me.

DEAN   No.

MARCUS   We've all been waiting for this.

BRYNN   Go ahead and read it, Amanda.

AMANDA   Okay. *(clears her throat)* Nash, Marcus and Dean, the friendships I have sustained with each of you over the years have been my lifeline. I flatter myself to think that when I am dead you will miss me. Of late, I have been assessing my life. Examining my actions, my work and my relationships. I will leave a number of novels behind and if they are remembered for even a generation I will be lucky. However, I think the true legacy a man leaves behind is the people who remember him. In a very real way each of you is my legacy. Therefore, I have decided to make it the mission of my next few years to find a way to give each of you exactly what you want. First, my material goods. The bed and breakfast I leave to— *(She stops.)* Bollocks.

NANCY   To who?

AMANDA   To my daughter Nancy Proctor and my companion Amanda Spencer—to be run or liquidated in whatever manner they choose.

NANCY   Whoa.

MARCUS   Don't stop reading just before he gets to me!

DEAN   Please, Amanda—go on.

AMANDA   Of course. To—to Nash Proctor I leave our daughter Nancy and my absence in her life. I know it's what you wanted. To Marcus Rogers I leave Brynn Gladstone. He is a worthy person and can be for you what I never could. To Dean Turnbull I leave Rhonda Brown. I can't condone what you need to do but I know you do need to do it. Good luck.

MARCUS   Brynn Gladstone?

BRYNN   Hold on.

AMANDA   I am writing this will on my forty-third birthday. If I have
         accomplished what I set out to do you will all be here now.
         If not, at least I tried. All of my money has been left to
         various charities and organizations. I learned a long time
         ago that unearned money will not bring happiness. I trust
         you will all understand. Love ya, mean it, Keith.

         Pause.

DEAN   You really did know him.

FRITZ   Everything I've told all of you is true.

NASH   Except your name?

MARCUS   That's right—RHONDA BROWN!

FRITZ   Don't be so melodramatic. What did you think I was going
         to do? Walk into a weekend with a bunch of artists and
         announce that I'm a film critic? I told a few white lies to
         keep the peace. Sue me. He was my friend.

MARCUS   Was he your friend too?

BRYNN   Yes. I met him at an art exhibition in London.

MARCUS   Were you lovers?

BRYNN   No. I admired him. He thought I was interesting. He told
         me a lot about Canada. He told me a lot about you. What
         a great friend you were.

MARCUS   He sent you to me?!

BRYNN   He just told me where to find you.

MARCUS   And you lied about your name?

BRYNN   I created a new identity.

MARCUS   Okay I'd kill for a joint right about now.

NASH   And what about you, Dean? Is Fritz your lover? Someone to
         replace your pretty Christian wife with?

DEAN Look, please—this is—it's crazy. People's dead friends don't do things like this in real life. They do it in movies or plays or—

AMANDA Books. This is exactly what would happen in one of his books.

MARCUS The bastard's writing our lives.

NASH Who is she, Dean? If this is some cheap affair after all of your God and family crap I'm going to be majorly PO'd.

DEAN She's not my lover. She's—she's—

NANCY She's what?!

FRITZ Go ahead and tell them.

DEAN Shut up!

FRITZ Tell them.

MARCUS Dean, it's okay.

NASH Trust us.

DEAN Fritz is here to castrate me.

Very long pause.

I can remember exactly when it started. I was building a model. One of those Aurora plastic model kits we got as kids. This one was the Frankenstein monster. He had a glow in the dark head. I was holding the monster's lower front torso. There were bits of plastic sticking up on the seams. I was cutting them off with an X-acto knife. The tube of glue was open and I was in this strange, dreamy state. In my body and out of it at the same time. My fingers were touching Frankenstein's crotch. It was slightly rounded and perfectly smooth. I felt the model piece with one hand and felt my own crotch with the other. Wilted hanging bits. Not smooth. Lumpy and real. Not hard and perfect like Frankenstein's. I pulled my shorts open and stared at myself. It was my balls. Not my cock. Just my balls—they were just—wrong. Wrong. I let the blade of the X-acto knife rest against the skin. I grabbed my scrotum and pulled it taut. I didn't really have to push down. I just ran it lightly along the flesh. The skin opened up so cleanly. There was no pain. For what seemed like a long time there was no blood. I was so close to getting at what was inside. But then there was blood and there was pain and maybe I made a noise or screamed or something because I looked up and my mother was standing in the doorway with a look frozen onto her face that I can't even begin to describe. My hands were covered with blood. I may have smeared some around my mouth. I fainted. Hospital. Doctors. Everyone blaming the airplane glue. No one really talking about it. It heals fast. The scrotum heals very fast. But ever since then. Like an obsession. A toothache. An itchy mole. They're not mine. They don't belong to me. I can't—it's like war veteran amputees describing phantom itch in reverse. I can't describe—they—they cause me pain—not physical pain—another kind of pain—in my brain. They're like tumours—growths—wrong—Do you understand?

> *Pause.*

MARCUS   No.

NASH   You're talking about mutilating yourself.

DEAN   It's like you knowing you're gay or—or being a transsexual. You have transsexual friends right? It's the way they talk about being women inside—

MARCUS   Yeah a woman inside a man. That's not a man with no balls.

DEAN   But it comes from the same place. There's no control.

NASH   And you're willing to put your position as an MP in jeopardy to have this operation?

DEAN   My family. Everything.

NASH   Why?

DEAN   Because—because I don't believe I am who God intended me to be.

BRYNN   Do you get off on this sexually?

DEAN   No. A bit. It's hard to explain.

BRYNN   *(to FRITZ)* And what about you? Does doing this turn you on?

FRITZ	No. I just like to cut people.
MARCUS	That makes perfect sense.
NASH	I need a drink.
NANCY	Mother.
NASH	One drink.
NANCY	Great.

NASH pours herself a drink.

NASH	Marcus?
MARCUS	No—I—should you drink?
NASH	Oh yes. So should you. We should all drink.
DEAN	Believe me. I don't want to be like this. If there were a way to turn it off—to make it stop—I'd do it.
NASH	Have you seen a therapist?
DEAN	Yes. I tried. I even went through an experimental form of aversion therapy.
MARCUS	Since none of us has any pot I will have a drink.
DEAN	I prayed. I meditated. I screamed and cursed God and cried. Sometimes it would fade. Kind of retreat. For years at a time. But it never really went away. It always came back. Stronger.
MARCUS	A big one.
DEAN	I thought I could arrange things so it would be possible to come here—have the operation—convalesce and go home without anyone ever knowing.
BRYNN	You can't be castrated without someone noticing. Your career—
DEAN	When was the last time you saw your MP's balls?
BRYNN	Your family—
FRITZ	When was the last time you saw your father's balls?
BRYNN	Your wife then.

DEAN   My wife knows about my condition.

NASH   Kelly approves of this?

DEAN   No. It's killing her. I know it's killing her. It's killing me too.

BRYNN   I might as well have a drink.

FRITZ   Women have their breasts removed or altered all the time. People remove moles, growths, tumours—unsightly third nipples. Nose jobs. Butt jobs. Circumcision.

AMANDA   I really—would—can I make anyone some tea? I'll make tea.

NANCY   Me too.

        AMANDA and NANCY exit.

DEAN   I know it's going to be hard for my family but if I were in an accident and lost an arm or a leg or an eye they'd still love me. They'd learn to live with it.

NASH   What do you think will happen if you don't do this, Dean?

        Pause.

DEAN   I don't know.

        Pause.

FRITZ   I can help him.

MARCUS   You don't perform surgery in a hotel room—not even a five-star hotel room.

FRITZ   I know what I'm doing.

MARCUS   Is the irony of being a film reviewer who also cuts off men's balls lost on you?

FRITZ   There are hundreds—maybe thousands of men like Dean. They get no sympathy and little practical help from the medical and psychiatric establishment. Especially since most of the men want to be conscious and drug-free during the procedure.

MARCUS   Shut up shut up shut up!

DEAN   It isn't real if I don't feel it.

NASH	And you've done this before?
FRITZ	I grew up on a ranch in Montana. The only child of one of the biggest ranchers in the state. We castrated my first kitten with a pair of tin snips and a Bic lighter when I was thirteen. We did my first dog when I was sixteen. I grew up branding cattle and gelding steers. I've taken a number of first aid and trauma treatment courses. I worked as a receptionist in a doctor's office for years before I became a full-time critic.
MARCUS	Have you ever done it to a person?
FRITZ	Five times in the last seven years.
NASH	I need another drink. Marcus?
MARCUS	Fill 'er up.
FRITZ	I'm very good at what I do.

NANCY and AMANDA enter.

AMANDA	I've made some tea.
NANCY	It's there. C'mon this shit's way too weird for me.

AMANDA and NANCY exit.

NASH	Dean, do you really want Fritz to do this thing to you?
DEAN	I don't—I don't know—I've prayed. I've prayed so much— but nothing changed.
FRITZ	I knew you didn't have the guts.
BRYNN	I hardly think it's guts that makes a man want to neuter himself.
FRITZ	He's transforming. Something you seem to know a bit about yourself.
MARCUS	Exactly.
BRYNN	I don't think we need to discuss that right now.
DEAN	I should go.
NASH	No. Please, Dean. Stay with us. Have a drink.
DEAN	I don't drink.

NASH	Start.
FRITZ	You really are the most amusing group of people I've ever met.
NASH	Clearly your lack of creativity and imagination has damaged you somehow.
FRITZ	How do you know I'm not creative?
NASH	Creative people don't have to do the kind of things you do—they can imagine them.
DEAN	What is this?
NASH	Who cares? Drink it.
FRITZ	You're just upset because I'm not a mindless fan of your work.
NASH	Your opinion means nothing to me.
FRITZ	Then why do you dislike me so much?
MARCUS	Because you're far too pretty and intelligent for the average person to be able to relate to.
NASH	You have to cut people to make them feel something for you. People only notice you if you hurt them! You're sick!
FRITZ	And what's Dean then?
NASH	Sick.
DEAN	That's right.
NASH	But he's our friend. We take care of our sick friends.
FRITZ	Yesterday none of you could stand him.
NASH	You don't know a thing about friendship.

Short pause.

Maybe you should leave.

FRITZ	Dean wants me here.
MARCUS	Does he?

Pause.

FRITZ   There's the most lovely crunching sound. Like celery with skin. That last man I did—in Portland Oregon—said it was like losing a weight that had been dragging him down for his entire life.

NASH   Think of your family.

FRITZ   He still emails me. He says his wife has finally accepted it and they couldn't be happier.

NASH   It's too drastic, Dean.

FRITZ   Choose.

Pause.

DEAN   I think you'd better go, Fritz.

FRITZ   It'll never go away.

DEAN   Please don't.

FRITZ   Every day it'll be there. Every day.

MARCUS Just get the hell out!

FRITZ begins to exit, then stops.

FRITZ   Marcus—and I mean this in the most constructive way—change your image. The eighties are over.

MARCUS Lick me.

FRITZ   And Nash—no offence but each of your films have shown a progressively weaker directorial hand. All the best with the wedding.

FRITZ exits.

MARCUS It's not too late to kill her.

NASH   Never mind. She'll be forgotten fifteen minutes after she stops writing.

DEAN   I'm sorry.

BRYNN   Imagine how desperate the press back in Canada would be for this information.

NASH   Don't even think about it.

BRYNN   He attacked us.

DEAN I had to say those things. People expect it. I'm sorry. I really am. If I could go back and change things I would. I really would.

MARCUS Do you promise to struggle for a world where all people are equal and to use whatever powers you possess for good and not evil?

DEAN Yes.

MARCUS Then it's over.

BRYNN Marcus you can't—

MARCUS Let it go.

Pause.

DEAN I hoped you'd understand—

MARCUS I don't understand, Dean. Really. I'm working like crazy to wrap my head around it because I know we all are who we are and do what we do and no one has the right to judge— but Jesus—this is really weird. It's—you're talking about your balls. You're talking about what makes us men, Dean. I'm sorry but I can't understand a man not wanting to be a man. A whole man.

NASH Dean, come with me.

DEAN Where?

NASH I'll tuck you in.

NASH leads DEAN off.

BRYNN This changes nothing.

MARCUS This changes everything.

Lights rise on NANCY's room. NANCY's suitcase is open on the bed and she's throwing clothes into it.

AMANDA Calm down.

NANCY People downstairs are seriously debating recreational castration. My mother's drinking again and the father I never knew just left me—

AMANDA Half of this business.

NANCY	You can have it.
AMANDA	I'm sure I can arrange some kind of buyout—it will take some time—
NANCY	No prob. Do what you can.
AMANDA	Although—
NANCY	What?
AMANDA	Nothing.
NANCY	What?
AMANDA	It's a very large house.

Pause.

NANCY	You want me to stay?
AMANDA	I didn't say that.

Pause.

NANCY	I am looking for a reason to get out of school.

Pause.

If you're doing this because you think I'm a lesbian I think it's only fair to let you know that's still very much—undecided.

AMANDA	I don't give a toss if you're a lesbian. I haven't had my period in five weeks.

Pause.

NANCY	What are you gonna do?
AMANDA	I don't know a lot of people—I don't really fancy my family much—
NANCY	Do you want me to stay and help you?
AMANDA	I could never ask that—
NANCY	It's cool. Canadians like to do nice stuff.
AMANDA	You're very kind.
NANCY	But don't go thinking I'm a replacement for the mythical Keith or whatever. I'm not like him.

AMANDA   You are a bit.

NANCY   Really?

AMANDA   Yeah.

>   *NANCY closes her suitcase.*

NANCY   What if we can't get along or have annoying habits that drive each other nuts?

AMANDA   I'm willing to see what develops.

NANCY   That's kinda scary.

AMANDA   Yes. I don't want anyone else to know. I don't need a lot of concerned godparents trying to help me out. I want this kid to grow up outside of anyone's shadow.

NANCY   Amen to that.

>   *Lights rise on the living room. MARCUS is nursing his drink. BRYNN is sipping his tea.*

MARCUS   The truth. Unvarnished please.

BRYNN   I come from a great deal of money.

MARCUS   Seriously?

BRYNN   Enough to keep both of us in the manner to which we are accustomed for a very long time.

MARCUS   And you never told me this because—?

BRYNN   Because it always complicates things. And because Keith dared me to give it all up—he said I'd never be the person I need to be if I didn't know how to support myself.

MARCUS   Other lies?

BRYNN   When I said I had sex with other men before you.

MARCUS   You're straight?!

BRYNN   No I've always been bi. On the inside. But I wasn't practicing.

MARCUS   You never slept with Boy George, Jimmy Summerville or George Michael?

BRYNN   No, but I have slept with Lisa Stansfield, Kylie Minogue and Gerri Halliwell.

MARCUS   Those nights you didn't come home—I always just assumed it was men.

BRYNN   I do still want to marry you.

MARCUS   Why? So you can take care of me the way Keith wanted you to.

BRYNN   So I can take care of you the way I want to.

MARCUS   I don't need taking care of.

BRYNN   You don't even know your postal code.

MARCUS   I always survive Brynn.

BRYNN   I enjoy being with you so much.

MARCUS   That marriage proposal really made me think. I mean marriage—that's ultimate sharing, right? Whatever's mine is yours. Whatever's yours is mine. What we really feel. What we really think. What we hope for. What we're afraid of. My joy. Your joy. My pain. Your pain. It's only gonna work if both parties open themselves up to trust and be trusted—

BRYNN   I do trust you.

MARCUS   But I don't trust you. You hurt me, Brynn. Every time you sleep with someone else—

BRYNN   You always said our relationship wasn't about monogamy.

MARCUS   Only because I knew it was impossible for you to be faithful.

BRYNN   But I can be faithful. I can change—

MARCUS   Have you ever had a successful monogamous relationship with a female?

BRYNN   No.

MARCUS   You want a relationship but you don't want to have to give anything up.

BRYNN   What are you talking about? I gave up who I was.

MARCUS   But you didn't give up what you do.

BRYNN   I hoped it would be different with men.

MARCUS   Not with this man.

> *Pause.*

BRYNN   Don't you dare dump me. I always get dumped and it's undeserved. I'm the guy. The perfect mate—excellent husband material—I'm bright. I'm handsome. I have the teeth. I have the hair. I'm charming but supportive. Interesting but not too high maintenance. I look good in press photographs. I can talk to anyone. I'M RICH.

MARCUS   I'm sorry.

BRYNN   You have no money. No career. No prospects.

MARCUS   I'll be all right.

BRYNN   You have no one to turn to.

MARCUS   You'll be okay.

BRYNN   I'll miss you so much. Please Marcus—

MARCUS   Look dumping someone is actually a lot harder than being dumped so please don't make it any more difficult. There are just too many lies.

BRYNN   I wasn't lying when I said I loved you.

MARCUS   Neither was I. But I don't think we were speaking the same language.

> *Long pause.*

BRYNN   Would you like to have the ring?

MARCUS   No. Thanks.

BRYNN   I'll move my things to another room until we fly out tomorrow.

> *Pause.*

MARCUS   Okay.

> *Pause. BRYNN exits. Lights rise on NASH and DEAN in DEAN's room. NASH is drunkenly trying*

> *to tuck DEAN into bed, while he keeps squirming to*
> *get away from her.*

NASH   Okay Dean—so here's the thing. No matter how normal we
look on the outside we're all weird somehow on the inside.

DEAN   Nash this isn't helping—

NASH   It stems from your hatred of sex.

DEAN   I'm sure they're connected.

NASH   And you only hate sex because that frigid bitch you
married—sorry—Kelly—doesn't know how to be a real
woman.

DEAN   It's not Kelly's fault.

NASH   We didn't have any problems.

DEAN   We only had sex once.

NASH   And you loved it!

DEAN   I was young.

NASH   I know exactly what you need.

> *NASH exposes her breasts to DEAN.*

NASH   Remember these?

DEAN   Nash, it's not that you don't have beautiful breasts—

NASH   You cried the first time you kissed them. I remember the
feeling of your tears on my nipples.

DEAN   Please get off—

NASH   Your hands were shaking.

DEAN   It was years ago—

NASH   Shut up.

> *NASH grabs DEAN and kisses him forcefully. DEAN*
> *breaks away desperately.*

DEAN   *(screams)* No!

> *Pause.*

NASH   I'm sorry.

DEAN   Do you think it's that simple?

NASH   I'm really sorry. I'm sorry. Keith, I'm sorry.

DEAN   I'm Dean.

Short pause.

NASH   I'm sorry, Dean.

MARCUS enters.

MARCUS   I heard someone scream.

DEAN   It was nothing.

NASH   Oh shit!

NASH races off to the bathroom.

MARCUS   Nash? *(to DEAN)* What did you do to her?

DEAN   It was me that screamed.

MARCUS   Oh.

Sound of NASH throwing up.

You all right in there?

NASH   *(off)* Fine. Don't open the door.

DEAN   I don't think the liquor was a good idea.

MARCUS   Liquor isn't ever about being a good idea.

DEAN   Keith bought me my first drink.

MARCUS   I think Keith's the reason for your other problem too.

DEAN   What?

MARCUS   Now I want you to keep an open mind here—you're not going to like some of things I'm going to say, but I think I have to say them. I've been thinking about what you said about losing your virginity during university and all of that. *(MARCUS has moved quite close to DEAN now.)* It was Keith who started that whole thing if you remember— teasing us all—daring us to get involved—and I know how much you cared for Keith—very very much—and since you've always been so hung up about homosexuality and since so much of the relationship us guys had was completely homoerotic— *(MARCUS touches DEAN's body.)* —well it seems to me maybe you repressed those completely natural feelings and—over the years—they evolved into something ugly and destructive. But it doesn't have to be. *(MARCUS slips his hand down the front of DEAN's pants.)* I think you can beat this terrible compulsion if you talk to a really good psychotherapist and give in to who you really are.

> *Pause.*

Why aren't you hard?

> *DEAN removes MARCUS's hand from inside his pants.*

DEAN   Because I'm not gay.

MARCUS   Really?

> *NASH enters from the bathroom.*

NASH   *(to MARCUS)* I just tried that, Marcus. Don't humiliate yourself.

DEAN   After what we did that night—my balls got stronger. They kept—asserting themselves. Through the alcohol—my time with Kelly—when my girls were born. It was like they were on fire.

MARCUS   But you're not going to do it now. With Fritz—Rhonda— the evil woman—whatever her name is.

DEAN   No. It's too—irresponsible. I have to involve Kelly in the process.

NASH   And if she doesn't want to be involved?

DEAN   I guess I can retire from politics and do it quietly. Go back to accounting. No one cares if an accountant has balls.

MARCUS   I think it's preferable actually.

DEAN   Marcus, please stop saying stupid things to disguise your discomfort.

MARCUS   I feel like puking just thinking about it.

> *Pause.*

DEAN   Whatever—whatever I do—whatever my ultimate decision is—I need to know that someone—someone still wants to know me.

                Pause.

                Nash?

                Pause.

NASH   Dean—please understand—they start to hack away at us soon enough—I can't—can't understand how anyone could mutilate themselves like that voluntarily. I can't.

DEAN   Marcus?

MARCUS   Everything about you is a lie. It always has been.

DEAN   I want to change that.

MARCUS   You're at least one lesbian foster mother too late.

DEAN   Are we still friends?

                Long pause.

MARCUS   No.

                MARCUS exits. NASH moves to DEAN, touches his shoulder gently and leaves. Lights rise on the dining area, very dimly. BRYNN sits silently at the table nursing a drink. AMANDA enters in her dressing gown.

BRYNN   Hello.

AMANDA   Can I assume that things didn't go so well with the fiancé?

BRYNN   Yes.

AMANDA   You should go to bed.

BRYNN   I was in bed. The orange room was too—orange.

                Pause.

AMANDA   Would you like some tea?

BRYNN   I'm fine.

AMANDA   You don't look fine.

BRYNN	I'm not.

BRYNN begins to cry.

AMANDA	Oh now. It's. Don't.

AMANDA moves to BRYNN and holds him as he cries. She rocks him and makes soothing sounds. Eventually BRYNN's crying fades although he stays in AMANDA's arms. After a moment, he tries to kiss her. She moves away from him.

BRYNN   It would make me feel better.

AMANDA   No. It would just make you feel different.

Pause.

BRYNN   You're right. I'm sorry. You're right.

AMANDA   It's okay.

Lights rise on NASH undressing for bed in her room. The door opens and NANCY enters.

NANCY   Are you still drunk?

NASH   I think I threw it all up.

NANCY   Okay then before anyone else's drama gets in the way I have to tell you I'm not going back to Canada, I'm not going to university and I'm not going to be a doctor.

Pause.

NASH   You're going to stay here.

NANCY   Yes.

NASH   It's so far away.

NANCY   I can fly home pretty much anytime. It's not such a big deal.

NASH   It's a big deal to me.

NANCY   Why?

NASH   Because things are changing—

NANCY   Yes. And for once they're not just changing for you.

NASH   I need you, baby—

NANCY   You need me to schlep around to your next film set so
            everyone can see what a fabulous down-to-earth REAL
            relationship we have. You need me around so I can listen to
            you complain or scream about the cast and the crew—you
            need me to be the best friend you lost in university and
            I don't want to do it anymore. I'm sorry. I don't. I want to
            be your daughter. The one who grew up and moved away.

                    Pause.

NASH   Of—of course. It's completely natural you'd want to assert
            yourself now. I understand—but right now—

NANCY   I want to stay here with Amanda. We're gonna try to run
            the place on our own.

                    Pause.

NASH   Good for you.

                    Pause.

NANCY   Get some sleep.

NASH   You too.

                    *NANCY exits. NASH is about to get into bed when
                    there is another knock at the door.*

            Yes?

                    MARCUS enters.

MARCUS   Pajama party sequel?

NASH   Sure. Do you think he'll be okay?

MARCUS   No. Nash about last night—

NASH   It was lovely. Thank you. Exactly what I needed. I don't
            have a high expectation for a repeat performance, and I'm
            sure you'll be very relieved to hear that.

MARCUS   Well yes.

                    NASH embraces MARCUS.

NASH   I'm sorry I abandoned you.

MARCUS   Hey, our break-up gave me my first solo album. And "Buzz Saw Affection".

NASH   You never told me that.

MARCUS   Nope. *(short pause)* I broke it off with Brynn.

NASH   I couldn't tell Nancy.

MARCUS   You can't go through this alone.

> *Pause.*

NASH   I know.

> *Pause. NASH looks to MARCUS. MARCUS looks away as the lights fade. Lights rise on the living/ dining area. AMANDA is cleaning up from the night before, singing quietly to herself. NANCY is laying out tea and croissants.*

NANCY   I forgot the milk.

AMANDA   Blue label in the fridge.

NANCY   Right.

> *NANCY exits.*

AMANDA   You'll have to rummage around a bit.

> *BRYNN enters.*

Good morning.

BRYNN   You're in an inappropriately good mood.

AMANDA   Don't think me rude but there are more high-maintenance people here than I could possibly maintain.

BRYNN   True.

AMANDA   Burying Keith today is like a whole new beginning.

BRYNN   What will you do now?

AMANDA   I'm thinking about attending university. Or maybe writing a book. Have you decided what you're doing?

BRYNN   Thought about it most of the night actually.

> *NANCY enters with milk.*

NANCY   And?

BRYNN   I'm hoping you'll let me stay.

                    Pause.

AMANDA   Stay? Here?

BRYNN   Yes.

NANCY   What for?

BRYNN   I don't really have any place to go. And this is such a large
           house. I thought perhaps you'd like a man around for the
           tough physical bits.

NANCY   But you're loaded.

BRYNN   No. My father's loaded. I have whatever I can get for the
           ring and that'll be the last time I ever touch my trust fund.
           Truly.

                    Pause. NANCY and AMANDA share a look.

NANCY   Well you're not going to be much use for the next nine
           months?

BRYNN   Oh?

NANCY   She's got a bloody bun in the oven.

AMANDA   Nancy!

NANCY   This is a big mother house. We could use the help.

BRYNN   Congratulations.

AMANDA   Not a peep. We don't want the old folks to know.

BRYNN   I understand completely.

                    Short pause.

AMANDA   You'd end up thinking of us as your own little harem.

BRYNN   Quite the opposite. Although you're both free to think of
           me as your own little stud if you like.

AMANDA   It's a bad idea.

NANCY   Should we think it over?

BRYNN   At least consider it.

AMANDA	I'll consider it.
BRYNN	Excellent.
	MARCUS enters.
MARCUS	Morning.
NANCY	Hi.
MARCUS	(*to BRYNN*) You okay?
BRYNN	I'll live. How did you sleep?
MARCUS	Don't ask.
	NASH enters.
NASH	Good morning.
NANCY	Do you need anything? Are you packed?
NASH	All taken care of. Where's Dean?
AMANDA	Haven't seen him yet.
NASH	Has anyone checked on him?
	DEAN enters with luggage.
DEAN	Why would I need checking on?
NANCY	After last night's psycho-drama, are you kidding?
DEAN	My apologies everyone. I had no business dragging all of you into that.
NASH	That's what friends are for.
DEAN	Is it?
	Pause.
MARCUS	Will you ride to the funeral with us?
DEAN	No. I've made other arrangements. Thank you.
NASH	Are you sure? We don't mind.
DEAN	I won't be attending the funeral.
NASH	Why not?
	FRITZ enters.

FRITZ   Good morning. Please put the insults on hold. I'm only
            here for a moment.

MARCUS   *(to DEAN)* You're not serious?

DEAN   Don't concern yourself, Marcus.

FRITZ   Are you ready?

DEAN   Yes.

FRITZ   Just a minute.

            *FRITZ moves to the coffin and touches it briefly. She
            moves back to DEAN.*

            Okay.

DEAN   Once again, sorry if I ruined your getaway.

NASH   Dean—

DEAN   Please Nash—do you really think anyone cares about the
            castration of one minor Canadian MP?

            Pause.

NASH   I care.

DEAN   No you don't. You just want to stop me from doing it.

FRITZ   Come on, Dean.

            DEAN and FRITZ exit. Pause.

NANCY   Mom?

NASH   I'm okay.

NANCY   You're not going to start drinking again are you?

NASH   No. I think I have to get smashed once every couple of years
            just to remember how bad it is.

MARCUS   She won. They always win.

BRYNN   Dean made his own decision. There's nothing either of you
            can do.

NANCY   It's his body.

MARCUS   Right.

Pause.

NANCY   Marcus, did you trim your moustache?

MARCUS   I never had a moustache.

BRYNN   You cut your hair.

MARCUS   I washed my eyeliner off.

AMANDA   I knew something was different.

BRYNN   It's taken ten years off your look.

MARCUS   Have you decided what you'll do?

BRYNN   I'm hoping to work for Nancy and Amanda.

MARCUS   You're staying here?

NANCY   We're considering it.

BRYNN   Some honest work will be good for me.

NASH   It's not supposed to be like this.

MARCUS   Nash.

NASH   It should all be—happier! Not crazy. This isn't what we worked for. It can't be.

NANCY   I'm coming home with you.

NASH   No. No! I'm okay. Sorry. I just—I'm fine.

NANCY   I don't think I should leave you alone.

MARCUS   Nash is coming to Toronto with me to put my penthouse up for sale.

NASH   I am?

MARCUS   You are.

NASH   Where will you live?

MARCUS   I've always loved that big old house of yours.

NASH   Really?

MARCUS   There's room for both of us.

BRYNN   What will you do on Vancouver Island?

Short pause.

MARCUS Write some more songs. Talk to Nash about ideas I have for movies. Sleep. That is of course if Nash will have me.

NASH You're sure?

MARCUS Hello. I'm homeless and washed-up. I need a friend.

NASH Me too. Thanks.

NANCY Shouldn't we get going?

AMANDA Right away.

BRYNN At least it's a sunny day. A rainy English funeral would've been too clichéd.

Pause.

MARCUS It was the Doug and the Slugs concert at the bar at the U of A.

NASH That's right. The place was packed and we just ended up at the only empty table left.

MARCUS I was wearing a leopard print shirt and wrap around sunglasses—Nash was in this rubber top and bondage pants—Dean was such a geek with his white shirt and his skinny tie that we didn't know whether he was a Mormon or a new wave rock critic.

NASH Keith was walking past the table—he was already drunk— baggy jeans, shirt untucked in the back, all that hair falling in front of his face—he saw us and stopped in disbelief. Came up to the table and said we were the unlikeliest threesome he'd ever seen and insisted on buying us all beer.

MARCUS If he hadn't done that we'd probably never have spoken to each other. I wonder what would've happened if we'd left that concert without speaking to each other.

NANCY Alternate universe and time continuum paradoxes give me a headache.

MARCUS What was he thinking?

BRYNN We'll never know.

NASH I miss him.

MARCUS	Me too.
NASH	And Dean. Poor Dean.
MARCUS	Dean.

Pause.

BRYNN	I'll check on the cars.
AMANDA	I'll come.

BRYNN moves to MARCUS.

BRYNN	Take care of yourself.
MARCUS	This story's not over yet.
BRYNN	I know.

BRYNN and MARCUS kiss quickly.

AMANDA	Nice to have met you all.
NASH	Thanks so much for your hospitality, Amanda. I know this must seem like a freak show to you—
AMANDA	Well yes—but I did live with Keith so it wasn't entirely unexpected.
MARCUS	You've handled yourself very well.
AMANDA	I had a good teacher. *Bon voyage.*
NANCY	Wait up guys.

AMANDA and BRYNN exit.

Take care of her.

NANCY kisses MARCUS quickly.

MARCUS	No prob.

NANCY faces NASH.

NANCY	I'm not abandoning you. You're a grown up.
NASH	That's right.

Pause.

NANCY	This doesn't mean I don't love you.

NASH   I know.

>   *They embrace fiercely. NANCY exits.*

MARCUS   You never told her.

NASH   The time's not right.

MARCUS   There's no good time for bad news.

NASH   I know.

>   *MARCUS and NASH move to either side of the coffin.*

>   You're sure you want to get involved in this, Marcus?

MARCUS   I'm here for you. In sickness and in health.

NASH   In sickness and in health.

MARCUS   With our addictions and our diseases.

NASH   Whatever new nightmare the future might hold.

MARCUS   You and me.

>   *Pause.*

NASH   Can we pray? I'd like to pray.

MARCUS   Me too.

>   *NASH lays one hand on KEITH's coffin, MARCUS lays his hand over hers, they share a look. Pause. NASH and MARCUS close their eyes and begin to pray silently. Slow fade to black.*

photo by David Hawe

Brad Fraser has written and directed for stage, screen, radio, television and print media. He plays include *Unidentified Human Remains and the True Nature of Love, The Ugly Man, Wolfboy, Poor Super Man, Martin Yesterday* and *Snake in Fridge.* His first film "Love and Human Remains" was directed by Denys Arcand. The second "Leaving Metropolis" was Brad's directorial film debut. Awards include a Genie for best adapted screenplay, The Los Angeles Critics Award, The Manchester Evening News Award, The Sydney Gay and Lesbian Film Festival Audience Favourite Award and two Chalmers Awards. Brad spent three seasons as producer/writer on "Queer as Folk" and he is currently developing a number of new projects for various media. He divides his time between Toronto and Los Angeles.